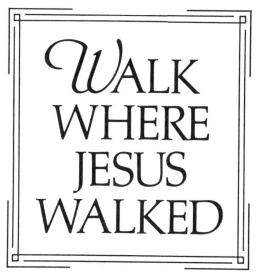

WALK WHERE JESUS WALKED

*A pilgrim's guide with
prayer and song*

Willard F. Jabusch

AVE MARIA PRESS
Notre Dame, Indiana

Library of Congress Catalog Card Number: 86-71224

International Standard Book Number: 0-87793-339-1

Book design and art: Elizabeth J. French

Photography:
Gary Boyd, 141; Byron Broudy, 11, 18, 46, 196, 199; Joseph
DeCaro, 54, 75, 117, 135, 150, 161, 174, 178, 188, 191;
Israeli Tourist Bureau, 40, 90; Robert Maust, cover, 9;
Richard Nowitz, 20, 29, 33, 35, 58, 65, 68, 72, 82, 86, 92,
96, 100, 105, 111, 122, 125, 138, 144, 147, 166, 171;
Religious News Service, 115, 158, 184.

Printed and bound in the United States of America

For my niece
Christi Marie Rankin

The **Rev. Willard F. Jabusch** is a professor of Homiletics and Chairperson of the Pastoral Ministry Department at St. Mary of the Lake Seminary in Mundelein, Illinois. A native of Chicago, he holds advanced degrees from the Seminary, Loyola University and a Ph.D. in Speech from Northwestern University. He has also done post-doctoral study at the Ecumenical Center in Tantur, Israel. His published books include *Singing His Story* (Musica Pacis, 1985), *The Person in the Pulpit* (Abingdon, 1980), *A Heritage of Hymns* (World Library, 1980) and *Look for the Lord* (Pastoral Arts, 1983). He is a composer of popular hymns and articles for such periodicals as *Catholic Digest, Commonweal, Chicago Studies, America* and *National Catholic Reporter.*

Contents

Foreword

Pilgrimages have been a constant element of our Christian heritage from the earliest days to the present. In the Western hemisphere, Catholics frequent such shrines as Ste. Anne de Beaupre north of Quebec City or the Basilica of Our Lady of Guadalupe on Tepeyac Hill outside Mexico City. Catholics from around the world make pilgrimages to Lourdes, Canterbury and Czestochowa. They journey to Rome to pray at the tombs of the Apostles Peter and Paul.

Throughout the history of Christianity the most popular place of pilgrimage has been the Holy Land and the sites made sacred by their association with Jesus and his first disciples. Indeed, the Holy Land has been close to the heart of our Jewish and Muslim brothers and sisters as well. There has always been a persistent desire to visit Jerusalem and the other holy places of pilgrimage.

Pilgrims to the Holy Land today, by their encounter with other visitors from around the world, have an opportunity to experience a much larger community of faith than they may have experienced before. Knowing that millions of Catholics and other Christians have visited these places during the past two millennia, contemporary pilgrims also experience a strong bond with the Church of the past and its diverse traditions.

Nevertheless, there are obstacles to making an authentic pilgrimage in the Holy Land today. The danger of violence in that volatile part of the world prompts caution and prudence. There is also the pervasive tourism and commercialism often associated, unfortunately, with holy places.

Pilgrims visit holy places not primarily to capture them for memory with camera shots from various angles, or to gawk with the curiosity of someone seeing an exotic place for the first time, or to go on an expensive shopping spree in a foreign land. A pilgrimage is a *spiritual* journey. Pilgrims visit the Holy Land to draw closer to the Lord, to become more deeply aware of what it means to be his disciples.

Pilgrimages, in other words, are special times of prayer and reflection. In this thoughtful book Father Jabusch skillfully guides pilgrims through the various holy places where Jesus lived with helpful directions and brief historical notes. More importantly, he suggests appropriate approaches to prayer — and singing — that will be of great profit to serious pilgrims. He also provides realistic suggestions about how to cope with the distractions of tourism and consumerism which are part of daily life — even for pilgrims!

This is not a guidebook on where to stay, where to dine, or where to shop. It is a handbook for those who seek an authentic pilgrim experience in the Holy Land.

JOSEPH CARDINAL BERNARDIN

ONE

Stories, Songs, and the People You Meet

The Stories

Story is piled upon story and century upon century in the Holy Land. For it is an ancient land, this bit of semi-tropical coastal plain which would compare, in size, with New Hampshire. Its ten thousand square miles include barren hills and desert, mountains and fertile valleys.

People had settled here, between the Jordan River and the Mediterranean Sea, long before Abraham who lived between 2000 and 1500 B.C. This land was a convenient bridge between Asia and Africa. If not exactly a "land flowing with milk and honey" it was, as the followers of Moses found, certainly more attractive than the wilderness of Sinai and the grim mountains of Moab.

The fierce Joshua, the successor of Moses, brought the Israelites here about 1300 B.C. But

Holy Land terrain

even before that, army after army swept across this coveted land, burning the camps of enemies, looting and killing. Survivors stumbled away to slavery in distant kingdoms. New masters ruled over the city-states and petty fiefdoms here.

About 1000 B.C., David, the shepherd king, seized Jerusalem as his capital and installed the Ark of the Covenant there. Tribes of nomads pastured their sheep and goats on the surrounding hills—as they do today—and prayed beneath the desert sky.

Later, the star of great Assyria rose and fell over this land. Then that of mighty Babylon. In 538 B.C., the Jews were allowed to return from their Babylonian exile by Cyrus, king of Persia. He made Palestine another minor province of his own vast empire.

In the year 331 B.C., Alexander the Great, the young military genius from Macedonia, put a sudden end to the Persian Empire. But young Alexander, already worshipped as a god, was decidedly mortal. When he died in 323 B.C., his own short-lived empire was carved up by his generals. Several centuries of turmoil followed during which Greek culture had a pervasive influence all over this area.

In their land, devout Jews were not impressed with white marble temples dedicated to worldly Grecian gods or with theaters ringing to the musical lines of Euripides and Aristophanes. Nor did naked athletes taking their exercise in the elegant new gymnasia capture Jewish support. When the Jewish temple was plundered in l69 B.C. and ancient traditions were violated, the Jews were outraged. In 167 B.C., three Maccabean brothers at last led a revolt which led to both religious and political freedom and to a new

The Holy Land

at the Time of Jesus

Sidon

SYRIA

Mt. Hermon ▲

PANEAS

• Caesarea Philipp

PHOENICIA

Tyre

ULATHA

GAULANITIS

GALILEE

Chorazin

Capernaum • Bethsaida

Ptolemais •

Magdala

Cana

Sea of Galilee

Mt. Carmel ▲

Tiberias

Hippos

Nazareth

▲ Mt. Tabor

Nain

• Gadara

Caesarea

Scythopolis

DECAPOLIS

Salim

Mediterranean Sea

Plain of Sharon

SAMARIA

Sebaste •

Mt. Ebal ▲

Jacob's Well

Mt. Gerizim ▲ Sychar

Jordan River

• Antipatris

Alexandrium

PEREA

• Arimathea

Joppa •

• Lydda

Emmaus •

Jericho •

Jerusalem • •

Bethany

Bethlehem •

Kh. Qumran

JUDEA

Herodium

Hebron •

Dead Sea

• Gaza

Masada •

NABATEA

IDUMEA

Beersheba •

Jewish dynasty. Then, in 63 B.C., Palestine fell under the yoke of Rome.

At first, it suited the interests of the Roman Caesar to allow this Jewish kingdom to prosper. Rome especially appreciated the pro-Roman feelings of King Herod the Great who reigned from 37 to 4 B.C. They allowed this cruel but competent Jewish king to rule his buffer state. His sons, however, were inept. By A.D. 6, it was necessary for Rome to take direct control. A procurator responsible to Caesar was installed in the port city of Caesarea. Political authority was in his hands and he would make regular official visitations up to Jerusalem with a suitably impressive battalion of Roman troops. It was, of course, during one of these visitations at a potentially explosive Passover time that a young Jew known as Jesus of Nazareth was condemned to crucifixion by the imperial representative in Palestine. And nothing would ever be quite the same again.

In A.D. 70, Jerusalem and its beautiful temple were destroyed by furious Roman forces. They wanted to crush the spirit of the unruly Jews. More than a century after Christ, the emperor Hadrian finally razed the city completely and built a new Roman town on its ruins. Even the name was changed. Jerusalem became Aelia Capitolina. No Jews could live there.

But it was another Roman emperor, Constantine, who fostered a new interest in this ancient place. In A.D. 313, he legalized Christianity throughout the empire. Encouraged by his mother Helena, Constantine started building shrines over the places associated with the life of Jesus. These shrines were, in fact, great and beautiful churches. Pilgrims began coming from all parts of the empire to visit them and to pray where Jesus was born, died and rose again.

Hermits, monks and nuns arrived in large numbers, and under Byzantine rule, monasteries and churches flourished like spring flowers after a good rain. By the fourth and fifth centuries, the desert was actually crowded with those who would imitate the wilderness experience of Jesus and John the Baptist. Their caves, the mosaic floors of their ruined chapels and fragments of wonderful carved pillars are found everywhere in the Holy Land.

A Persian invasion in A.D. 614 destroyed a great number of churches. But it was really the followers of Mohammed thundering out of the Arabian desert with fire and sword who put an end to Christian control of the Holy Places. The caliph Omar conquered Jerusalem in A.D. 638 and a rich era of Christian building and devotion was over.

Pilgrims from Europe were allowed to come in discreet numbers until 1071. Then the Seljuk Turks occupied the Holy City and put an end to pilgrimage. Christian Europe was frustrated and angry. Thousands were ready to respond to the call of Pope Urban II. In 1095, he asked Christian Europe to free the Holy Places by a crusade "against the infidels."

Kings, princes and bishops led the young knights and squires of Europe in this First Crusade, this "holy war." On June 15, 1099, they entered Jerusalem and massacred all the inhabitants who followed Islam! Such atrocities are not easily forgotten.

Of course, not all crusaders were rogues and soldiers of fortune, fanatics and opportunists. Many were honest, devout Christians. Certainly they did not lack initiative and courage! Money and manpower from Europe built a whole "Latin Kingdom of Jerusalem." It boasted of Gothic castles, abbeys and cathedrals to rival those of France and England. Even in ruins, Crusader hilltop forts or underground storerooms cannot fail to impress modern visitors.

But ambitious construction projects were not enough to assure security for the Latin Kingdom. The Crusader knights were slaughtered by the clever Saladin in a great battle near the Sea of Galilee in 1187. The Crusaders held on to their last stronghold, the port of Acre (Akko) until 1291. The crusades, so noble in concept and so tragic in execution, were over. Numerous Romanesque and Gothic churches were destroyed or turned into mosques, and the great fortresses were left to crumble on their hilltops. For the next seven centuries, Palestine became a sleepy backwater province under Mamelukes from Egypt and later under the Ottoman Turks from Istanbul.

In the twentieth century, the Turks made the unhappy mistake of joining Germany and being defeated in the First World War. So Palestine was later taken from Turkey and given to Britain under a mandate of the League of Nations. Britain's Lord Balfour declared in 1917 that Jews would have a "national home" in Palestine, an unwelcome proposition for both the Moslem and Christian Arabs already living there.

But immigration of Jews into Palestine continued in substantial numbers throughout the 1920s and '30s. Some were fleeing the insanity of Hitler while others came from North and South America convinced that they should spend their lives in this new land helping "to make the desert blossom." The question remained however: Just whose desert was it? The Jewish Zionists bought land where they could. They planted citrus and almond groves, irrigated fields of strawberries and melons. They were able to turn acres of wasteland into "kibbutz" farms that produced three crops a year and supplied Europe with grapefruit, oranges, fresh flowers and vegetables.

But by 1948, Britain was weary of terrorist attacks on its soldiers and the mutual hatred of Arabs and Jews. It withdrew its forces and the new State of Israel came into existence on May 14, 1948. A strange and irregular frontier was established after an armistice with the Arab powers. Jerusalem, the capital, was a divided city. Bethlehem, Hebron, Jericho and Nablus belonged to the Kingdom of Jordan. The seacoast and most of Galilee belonged to Israel.

Another war in 1967 gave Israel everything west of the River Jordan, the so-called West Bank. Many Arabs fled their towns and the refugee camps that had been their homes since 1948. In Jordan, Syria and Lebanon young Palestinians joined the Palestinian Liberation Organization and began using terrorist techniques similar to those the more radical Zionists had used against the British.

And so, the land where Jesus lived remains a land of conflict. "Shalom" or "Peace," the common Hebrew greeting, continues to be a hope and not a reality.

Christian pilgrims to the Holy Land seem divided in their sympathies. Some find the Arab cause convincing; others are strongly pro-Israel. Most, I think, are confused by the complexities and the arguments, the propaganda, the hurts and the fears. Uniformed men and women are everywhere. You see them hitchhiking back to their units from their homes in Tel Aviv or Haifa, carrying their rifles as casually as tennis rackets. Security is very tight at Israel's airports and bus

Israeli soldiers

stations. There are many roadblocks and identity card checks. There seem to be an inordinate number of prisons for such a small country.

Although the pilgrim will suffer few inconveniences from any of this, to ignore the tension and anxiety would be foolish if not impossible. Prayers for forgiveness and peace have a special urgency in this climate of suspicion and hatred.

Both Jews and Arabs welcome the pilgrim. Both hope, I suppose, that the foreign visitor will return home with an appreciation of their pain and their desires, of the justice of their cause. How good it would be for all concerned, including pilgrims, to remember the words of Jesus: "Judge not and you will not be judged."

Christian pilgrims do not come to Israel to see the citrus groves or visit a kibbutz. Colorado has better mountains and Egypt and Greece have more impressive ruins. France and Italy have more glorious churches and Mexico and

China offer more varied and artistic handicrafts. Christian pilgrims come to visit the land where Jesus lived. By following in his earthly footsteps, they hope to follow him more closely in faith and love.

The Gospel message takes on a new immediacy and stronger color when one walks in the places where Jesus spoke and sees the landscapes that Jesus saw. In fact, the geography and local customs so influence some pages of the Bible that it is difficult to understand them without having seen this land.

But it is also vain for the modern visitor to be overly concerned about exact locations. It is just not possible, after almost two thousand years, to pinpoint a particular spot where some Gospel word was spoken or action took place. Most of the time, the evangelists were not concerned with giving precise information on places. They were preachers desirous of converting people to the way of Christ, not map makers or scientific historians.

As pilgrims today we depend therefore on ancient traditions. We must rely on the fact that our Byzantine and Crusader predecessors saw fit to build a shrine or a church at a certain place. Sometimes, in order to wipe out a primitive Christian veneration at a certain site, the pagan Emperor Hadrian constructed temples or statues at that location. As clues to authenticity, we also have the records of early European pilgrims and ecclesiastical writers, as well as the bits of mosaic, fragments of inscriptions and carved stones so dear to the archeologists.

We must frankly admit that we will never have perfect certainty about many "holy" places. Most of the time, we must be satisfied with a probability. We will be content to say that somewhere near these traditional sites, the life of Jesus was lived out in obedience and love.

Of course much has changed and much is changing in the Holy Land. Cars and buses are replacing donkeys and camels. Plush hotels take the place of pilgrim hostels and ancient caravansaries, inns where caravans stayed. Floodlights play on the walls of the Old City of Jerusalem today. Airlines bring in many more Christian pilgrims (and worldly tourists) than could ever have arrived on nineteenth-century ships from France and Russia.

Pilgrims on Via Dolorosa, Palm Sunday

But some things do not change. The harsh hills of Judea. Sunrise over the Mount of Olives. The serene beauty of the Lake of Galilee. We are all influenced by the climate, the topography, the trees and flowers, the customs and monuments of our homeland. And Jesus was surely influenced by his. It is good for us to walk under the same sort of cloud formations and see olive and fig trees like he saw. We can look out over the same wonderful lake he knew. It is possible to follow the same path he took from Bethany, over the Mount of Olives, down into the valley of Kidron and up to the gate of the Holy City.

What does it matter if it is not the exact gate which Jesus entered? Why should it bother us to know that the street level is much higher now than in the first century. Even the walls of Jerusalem were largely rebuilt in the sixteenth century.

What is important is that we are here in a very special country. We have come with humility and hope to draw closer to our dear Brother and Savior. We seek to hear his words with a new freshness and be confronted more directly with the challenge of his life, death and resurrection.

We are happy and honored to spend some days here in the very land where Jesus lived. We are here to learn, to pray and to experience the presence of one who is both Son of Man and Son of God.

And then, God willing, we will be ready to return to our homes with a new zeal and burning faith. For now, Our Lord's mission is surely our own.

The Songs

Just to talk with other pilgrims while on pilgrimage is important and powerful. Information is given and feelings are shared. If the talk is intense and if much metaphor is used the sharing may even be something like poetry.

But music goes still further. Communication receives a new dimension. It becomes more mysterious and more profound. When people sing together they enter into a sense of wonder and communion that moves them beyond words and concepts.

All singing binds people together. But when Christians sing their hymns, they reach out also to God and are one with the angels and saints.

Pilgrims in the land of Jesus should really sing. But their songs should not be difficult and, if possible, they should suit the place and the moment. Songs are provided in this book which can be quickly learned on the tourist bus or at the hotel after supper. (There is frankly very little to do in the Holy Land in the evening except have a songfest!)

The melodies are, for the most part, from folk hymns and songs. They have been polished smooth by centuries of loving use. They have a noble simplicity which makes them ageless and gives them an international appeal. If someone has brought along a guitar or flute, so much the better! And frequently there are a few folks with an aptitude for singing in harmony. But a simple and strong melody should have no trouble working on its own.

The day is past when English-speaking visitors stood back in silent awe while German or

French-speaking pilgrims vigorously sang their hymns. They have discovered that their prayers can also be carried up on the wings of music. Song expresses the pilgrim experience. In that very expression, the Holy Land experience becomes more profound.

But perhaps your group is very small and shy. Perhaps indeed you are by yourself and do not feel up to singing a solo! Then, the texts of the songs can be read aloud or silently. The harmonies that God composes in a humble heart are always the most beautiful.

Now Is the Moment

1. Now is the moment of our freedom; Now is the time to be reborn; For Christ has come, a sun to brighten A people saddened and forlorn.

2. Have you been burdened, heavy laden? He knows the grief that's in your heart His healing touch will cure all anguish Allow your life, at last to start!

Refrain

We have a God who loves us, His only son He gave; He came and suffered here among us, But then He rose from out the grave, He came and suffered here among us, But then He rose from out the grave.

Sea and Islands, All Are Laughing

1. Sea and is- lands, all are laugh- ing;
2. Fire will sweep and flash be- fore him;

Earth is glad with joy- ful cry.
En- e- mies will burn a- way;

God is King and lives in splen- dor
E- vil scat- ters in the whirl- wind;

Shout his name as he goes by!
Moun- tains melt like wax a- way;

Cloud and mist his throne en- fold;
He will rule from sea to sea;

Trum- pets thun- der bright and bold.
He will Lord and Mas- ter be.

Al- le- lu- ia, Al- le- lu- ia,

God, our God, is Lord and King!

3. Judah's cities shout their gladness; Lord, you are so good and great.
Zion's heard it: you are Savior, Freeing from a dismal fate;
All his loved ones will be free; God's own friends a light will see.

Psalm 97: 1-3, 5, 8-11
Traditional Slovak hymn tune
Copyright © 1979 by Willard F. Jabusch

The People You Meet

Jerusalem, the capital of Israel, is, of course, not nearly as big as Tokyo or Mexico City. Nor is it as cosmopolitan as New York or Geneva. Jerusalem does not have the Vietnamese of Paris, the Chinese of San Francisco or the Latinos of Los Angeles. Chicago has many more Blacks and London more Indians and Pakistanis. But, considering its rather modest size, there are few cities with such a variety of peoples and religions as Jerusalem.

Rome, of course, is also a great religious magnet but of a different sort. It does draw an exciting mix of peoples from all parts of the world, but they are almost all Catholics. They are loyal to the Pope and united in doctrine and discipline. Jerusalem is far more diverse!

The Jews follow the most ancient religious tradition found there. But they are deeply divided among themselves. The great majority do not observe the religious requirements. Others follow a middle-of-the-road approach and observe the major holy days. A smaller but highly influential group is strictly Orthodox. They have managed to promote some rather unpopular laws regulating what can and cannot be done on the Sabbath, which begins at sundown on Friday. Some Orthodox men can be seen wearing long black coats and fur hats. Boys have long side curls and the women cover their shaved heads with a kind of veil or scarf. Their clothes and customs are not much different from the Hasidic villages of Eastern Europe in the eighteenth century. These Orthodox young men and women are exempt from military service. Their unbending religiosity is resented by many other Israelis.

Many Arab men, on the other hand, can be distinguished just as easily as the Orthodox Jews. They wear a cloth worn over their heads which is often held in place by a band of thick cords. This headdress, which originated in the desert, is even used by many younger urban Arabs. Bedouin women are still seen in long dresses with intricate black and red designs. They wear heavy silver and amber jewelry. Their necklaces may be formed of old silver coins, which have been passed down in the family from Turkish days.

In the seventh century, most Arabs converted to Islam which had been founded by Mohammed in the early 600s. But not all have Mos-

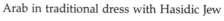

Arab in traditional dress with Hasidic Jew

lem roots. Some are Christians, either Catholic, Orthodox, or more recently, Protestant. Bethlehem, for example, is the home of many Christian Arabs.

Almost without exception, Arabs feel they are treated as second-class people by the Israeli government and, no matter what their religion, they are united in their opposition to the Jewish state. They are not allowed to join the Israeli army and some radical Jews like Rabbi Kehane want all of them driven from the country.

It is a fact that the Arab population is growing faster than the Jewish. There is a fear among Jews that if all Arabs are allowed to vote, they will take over the country in the future.

And in the Holy Land, Orthodox Christians are also commonly seen. In North America, most Catholics and Protestants have little or no contact with them.

By the middle of the eleventh century, after many years of slowly drifting apart, it was clear that Greek-speaking Christians of the East and the "Latins" of Italy and northern Europe no longer formed one church.

Although some, such as the church of the Ukraine, established contact with the pope, the bishop of Rome, and accepted his primacy, most Eastern churches did not, and generally considered themselves "Orthodox" (having the true faith). They are suspicious of the intentions of the "Catholic" (universal) religion centered in Rome. Mutual excommunications in 1054 and the vicious sack of Orthodox Constantinople by Catholic Crusaders in 1204 did not pour oil on the troubled waters.

In Jerusalem, therefore, it is possible to visit many Greek Orthodox churches and shrines as well as those of the Orthodox Armenians, Syrians, Coptic Egyptians and Ethiopians. Russian Orthodox establishments can also be found although Russian pilgrims no longer come. The Roman Catholic Church holds that all of these churches have valid sacraments but are in "schism" because they are not in union with the pope. They, in turn, feel that the Roman bishop has made unfounded claims, undermined ancient traditions, and that Catholics have diluted the true faith.

In fact, the Eastern churches do have rich traditions. The Mass of the Roman Church seems very simple and rather colorless when compared to the long, elaborate and highly "mystical" liturgies of the Oriental churches. Most of these follow the Rite of St. John Chrys-

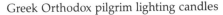

Greek Orthodox pilgrim lighting candles

ostom, bishop of Constantinople. They are meant to be a foretaste of heaven; they are unabashedly "other-worldly." The stylized painting of the icons, the clouds of incense, and the repeated chanting of litanies all bring the worshipper to a sense of adoration before the throne of God. In this tradition, there is no such thing as a "relevant guitar Mass!" In fact, not even an organ is allowed. And there are no women allowed in the sanctuary!

The North American Catholic or Protestant visitor at the Greek or Armenian Divine Liturgy may experience a definite culture shock in the Holy Land. But that does not mean that the opportunity should be missed. There will never be Christian unity until we come to know and respect each other.

Jerusalem is also a wonderful place to visit the smaller Oriental churches which again recognize the bishop of Rome. Yet they keep their own languages, liturgical rites, canon law and ancient customs. Theirs has not been an easy road. The Orthodox have considered them traitors for "going over" to union with Rome. The Roman authorities, on the other hand, have often been insensitive and suspicious of anyone so "strange." There have been attempts to Latinize them and test their loyalty. But these churches truly are a bridge toward unity.

The "mainline" Protestant churches are also all represented in and around Jerusalem. The fundamentalist churches and the Mormons are especially in evidence. However, the Jewish authorities were clearly concerned about the large and conspicuous piece of property that the Mormon followers of Joseph Smith and Brigham Young obtained on the slope of Mt. Scopus facing the city.

Outside of Jerusalem, pilgrims find that it is possible to meet Samaritans, who broke away from Judaism before Christ. There are also the Druse, who are considered heretics by other Moslems. And there are the Bahai, a group which broke more recently from Islam and which has its world headquarters in Haifa.

The pilgrim will learn that the entire Holy Land constitutes a living class in comparative religion! On any Sunday, it is possible to have a variety of religious experiences in Christian churches. Then, one can visit at the Western or Wailing Wall of the Jews and the Moslem mosque on the Temple platform.

It becomes evident that all these "children of Abraham"—Jews, Christians, Moslems—must learn to live in peace and forgiveness in this land which all consider "holy." If not, all of the varied prayers and rituals seem pretentious and vain.

A Pilgrim People

1. To be a pilgrim people in
   ev-'ry age and time,
   To join the poor and lowly in
   ev-'ry land and clime,
   We're called to follow Jesus, who
   had no home or bed,
   Who trav-eled down the highways, no
   place to lay His head.

2. We will not trust in princes, the
   rich who boast their worth,
   We will not gather into barns the
   treasures of this earth.
   Our lot is with the outcast, with
   all who mourn and weep,
   Who drag their painful crosses, and
   crowns of thorns must keep.

3. Then follow Christ where He may lead, then let Him be your guide.
   He came to save the little ones, He took the poor man's side.
   Though power, money, pleasure, may try to change your mind,
   Remember that His kingdom is of a better kind.

TWO

Jerusalem

The Walls and Gates of the City

The American is unaccustomed to walled cities like Avila in Spain, Rothenburg-on-the Tauber in Germany or Carcassonne in France. He or she may find that the proud walls of Jerusalem are among the most lasting memories of the Holy Land. The walls are truly splendid and now are dramatically illuminated at night. At a number of places, it is possible for the friskier pilgrim to climb up and walk along the top. The walls shape the Old City within and give an illusion of great antiquity. It is usually a disappointing surprise when pilgrims discover that they were built only in 1535-38 by the Ottoman Sultan Sulaiman, "the Magnificent." Only the "Tower of David," the lower levels of the Citadel near the Jaffa Gate, and the great stone blocks of the re-

Jerusalem from a distance

taining walls supporting the Temple terrace would have been seen by Jesus and the Apostles. They are from the elaborate building programs of Herod the Great.

In fact, Sulaiman followed the line of walls laid out for the Emperor Hadrian's rebuilt city of A.D.135 and not the outline of the city at the time of Christ. For this reason, Calvary and the Holy Sepulchre are within the walls rather than outside the city as the Passion narratives described them. On the other hand, Mount Sion and the Upper Room were not included within the area enclosed by Sulaiman's walls. To reach that area, one must leave the walled city of today through the war-scarred Sion Gate.

Beneath Sulaiman's splendid Damascus Gate, the rock and earthen rubble has been cleared down to the A.D.135 level. There, the gate of Hadrian's time was found. Gates used by Jesus can be seen beneath the temple terrace on the south and east sides. The "Golden Gate" also marks an ancient gate which once led down toward Gethsemane. All have been walled up for centuries. But the sixteenth-century gates such as St. Stephen's Gate, majestic and quiet, and the Damascus Gate, showy and crowded, are not unworthy successors.

Hail, Jerusalem!

And now our feet are standing
  in your gateways, Jerusalem.
Jerusalem restored! The city,
  one united whole!
Here the tribes come up,
  the tribes of Yahweh . . .
Pray for peace in Jerusalem,

"Prosperity to your houses!
Peace inside your city walls!
    Prosperity to your palaces!"
Since all are my brothers and
    friends,
    I say "Peace be with you!"
                (Psalm 122, 2-4, 6-8)

Let Us Pray Together

*Lord God of life, we join the thousands of pil-
grims, including Jesus himself, who have entered the
gates of Jerusalem with joy and expectation. But this
pilgrimage place has suffered. The veil of the Temple
was torn in two. And, as Jesus foretold, not a stone of
the Temple now stands upon a stone. Yet we recognize
that this city has been hallowed by the presence, by
the words and by the deeds of your only Son, Jesus
Christ. Bless us here. Open our minds and hearts to
your good inspirations. Help us to regain a sense of
awe before your beauty and majesty. For you are
"holy, holy, holy, Lord God of power and might," and
Jesus Christ is our Messiah, our King of Glory who
leads us home to you. Amen.*

The King of Glory

Refrain

The King of Glo-ry comes, the na-tion re-joic-es, O-pen the gates be-fore him, lift up your voic-es.

Verses

1. Who is the King of Glo-ry; how shall we call him? He is E-man-u-el, the pro-mised of a-ges.

2. In all of Galilee, in city and village.
   He goes among his people curing their illness.

3. Sing then of David's Son, our Savior and brother.
   In all of Galilee was never another.

4. He gave his life for us, the Lamb of salvation.
   He took upon himself the sins of the nation.

5. He conquered sin and death; he truly has risen.
   And he will share with us his heavenly vision.

Israeli folk song
Copyright © 1976, 1986 by Willard F. Jabusch

The Temple

About the year 1000 B.C., David captured Jerusalem from the Jebusites. He had an altar built there and placed the Ark of the Covenant nearby. The Ark contained the Tablets of the Law (2 Samuel 6). But the steep rock above the Kidron valley had already been made holy by the obedience of Abraham. It was there that he prepared to sacrifice his only son Isaac, but God gave him a ram to sacrifice instead (Genesis 22).

It was on this same rocky Mount Moriah that David's son Solomon built the first Temple with cedarwood from Lebanon, copper columns and gilded walls. For almost four hundred years, animals were brought to the Temple for sacrifices and prayers were constantly chanted in this sumptuous setting. The Temple was destroyed by the Babylonians in 587 B.C. but rebuilt by the Jews in a more modest style in 516 B.C. (Ezra 6: 3).

The Jewish King Herod later had the whole Temple complex enlarged and rebuilt in a splendid Graeco-Roman style. He was trying to win the loyalty of his subjects chafing under Roman rule. It was finished a short time before the birth of Jesus and was destroyed by the Romans in A.D. 70.

Josephus, the first-century Jewish historian, vividly described his impression of this magnificent building: "The outside of the Temple was a delight to the eye and to the heart. Sheathed in heavy gold plates on all sides, it shimmered in the gleam of the sunrise and matched the sun in its brilliance."

In A.D. 70, the angry Romans were not able

Part of the northern Old City wall

to destroy the enormous blocks of stone which
Herod used as walls to support the Temple.
These blocks remain to astonish us as they must
have astonished visitors at the time of Jesus. The
Western Wall provides today's Jews with a place
to pray close to their ancient temple. On a Friday
evening as the Sabbath begins, it is one of the
world's great sights to see hundreds of devout
Jews return to pray at the great stone wall. There
is often a fervor and prayerful ecstasy that is
quite alien to Anglo-Saxons.

But Jews cannot pray above where the Temple itself actually stood. The Temple square now
belongs to the Moslems. It is a holy place for
them because the seventeenth sura or chapter of
their Koran tells of Mohammed's miraculous
journey to Mount Moriah and his ascent from
there into the seven heavens.

In 691, the Caliph Abd el Malik finished the
extraordinary and beautiful "Dome of the Rock"
over the Moriah crest. His son then turned a
large church built by Justinian in honor of the
Virgin Mary into the famous El Aqsa Mosque.

Although Jews and Christians are now allowed to visit both buildings, the whole area remains under Islamic control.

But Jewish excavations continue around the walls on the south and east sides. Several important gates to the original Temple have been revealed as well as a monumental staircase and arches. To reach the crowded porch where he preferred to teach, Jesus and his apostles would have climbed this very staircase to enter the Temple area high above the valley.

Somewhere in the vast Temple square Jesus drove out the money changers and merchants who had made His Father's house "a den of thieves" (Mark 11; Luke 19).

The people of Israel were invited to go on pilgrimage up to the Temple at Jerusalem three times each year: Passover (Pesah), Pentecost (Shabhuoth), and on the Feast of Tents (Sukkoth). They came to rejoice before the face of the Lord God, to be delighted by the Divine Presence, to be full of hope in the All-powerful who loved them.

The Hebrews had come back from exile longing for the glory of God. They came out of the desert, thirsty as a deer who seeks living waters. As Scripture testifies, they sought the brightness of the holy city, yearning to enter Sion, "the house of prayer for the peoples" (Isaiah 56: 7).

> In the days to come
> the mountain of the Temple of
>   Yahweh
> shall tower above the mountains
> and be lifted higher than the hills.
> All the nations will stream to it,
> peoples without number will come to

it; and they shall say:
"Come, let us go up to the mountain
    of Yahweh,
to the Temple of the God of Jacob
that he may teach us his ways
so that we may walk in his paths:
since the Law will go out from Sion,
and the oracle of Yahweh from
    Jerusalem."

(Isaiah 2: 2-3)

Be glad and rejoice for ever and ever
    for what I am creating,
because I now create Jerusalem "Joy"
and her people "Gladness."
I shall rejoice over Jerusalem and
exult in my people.

(Isaiah 65: 18-19)

They went as a body to the Temple
    every day
but met in their homes for the
    breaking of bread;
they shared their food gladly and
    generously.

(Acts 2:46)

Let Us Pray Together

Lord Jesus, Mary and Joseph presented you in the Temple as a baby. Old Anna and Simeon rejoiced to see the day. Then you came here as a twelve-year-old to teach the elders and astonish them with your wisdom. And it was here in the crowded porches of the Temple that you later taught the people day by day about the kingdom of God. You told them that their God did not require bloody sacrifices of lambs and cattle. You reminded them instead of the importance of reverence and the primacy of the spiritual. The money changers who fled from you did not forget you. What you said and did in this Temple contributed to your condemnation.

Today, it is not this great pile of stone which is important; each of us now is a living temple. In each of us, you dwell with the Father and the Holy Spirit. You have made us more precious than the ancient Temple's marble or gold. We are now your dwelling place. Help us to be aware of your holy presence. Amen.

Jerusalem Is Fair

1. Je- ru- sa- lem is fair, God's glo- ry ev- 'ry- where! A home for king and pea- sant, for a- ges past and pres- ent, Je- ru- sa- lem is fair, God's glo- ry ev- 'ry- where!

2. How well the cit- y shines with gems of ma- ny kinds; A ri- ver thru it flow- ing and treas- ures past all know- ing, How well the cit- y shines with gems of man- y kinds.

3. Its gates will never close, no danger from our foes!
The saints will enter in there, no place for shame or sin there,
Its gates will never close, no danger from our foes!

4. God wipes all tears away, no death or pain can stay.
The old things now are going, a fresh new hope is growing;
God wipes all tears away, no death or pain can stay.

5. "Thanksgiving to the King," His saints will ever sing.
Each heavenly musician performs his composition,
"Thanksgiving to the King," His saints will ever sing.

Franconian melody
Copyright © 1976, 1986 by Willard F. Jabusch

Church of the Holy Sepulchre: Chapel of Calvary

Deep in the Old City is the most important church in the world for all Christians.

As we enter the Church of the Holy Sepulchre, we turn right and climb up the steep steps to the Chapel of Calvary. How can anyone describe the feelings this place evokes? The rock of Golgotha (the "skull"), which was the city's place of execution, still stands sixteen feet above floor level. Now, however, it is no longer outside in the open. The Crusaders enclosed it and made it a raised side chapel of the main church. Calvary is under cover.

Here again in this sacred spot we are reminded of the separations among Christians. The right side of the chapel constitutes the eleventh station of the cross where Jesus is nailed to the cross. This altar is in the custody of the Latin rite. The twelfth station of the cross just to the left is in the possession of the Greek Orthodox.

None of this will look to the pilgrim like a hill of execution or like any remembered picture of the crucifixion. Above the Latin rite altar is a modern and totally uninspired mosaic of the nailing to the cross. Above and around the Greek altar is an excess of lamps and icons. Under their altar is a hole through which the original rock can be touched. Between the two altars is still another and smaller altar with a Portuguese image of the Sorrowful Mother which marks the thirteenth station of the cross where Jesus was taken down from the cross.

Frankly, it can all be a disappointment for contemporary Christians. Many of us would prefer that the stark reality and profound meaning of the death of Jesus be presented in a different way. But tastes are certainly not universal!

We are indeed standing over the rocky outcropping that formed the place of the crucifixion.

Church of Holy Sepulchre exterior

Who can guess how much of the rock has been chipped away by pious visitors through the centuries?

In fact, the Crusaders even buried the European conquerors of Jerusalem in a chapel carved out of the rock below. It is a wonder, I suppose, that any of the rock of Golgotha is left at all.

Yet there can be little doubt that this is the place where Jesus of Nazareth hung for three hours in agony upon the cross. The site was, of course, known and apparently honored by the first Christians. All Jews, including Christian Jews, were driven out of the city after its destruction by the Roman general Titus in A.D. 70. But they quickly returned.

Calvary was outside of the city then, not within the walls as it is today. It was probably because of Christian veneration here that Emperor Hadrian decided to extinguish the devotion by erecting a temple of Venus on Calvary and one of Jupiter over the tomb. That, of course, only served to mark the sites more definitely for future Christians.

When Helena, the mother of Constantine, the first Christian emperor, arrived in Jerusalem in 326, Christian sites were rescued. Orders were given for the removal of the pagan constructions and the building of worthy shrines. Christians have been praying here ever since. Even after the Moslem conquest, Christians returned to the Church of the Holy Sepulchre. Persians destroyed most of the building in 614. And pilgrims came back again after this holy place was damaged by the insane Caliph El Hakim in 1009.

What we see today is substantially a Crusader church rebuilt in 1099 with some remaining elements from the churches of Constantine and Justinian. Repairs are almost constantly in progress. The sound of hammering mingles with the chants of Latins, Greeks, Armenians and Coptic Egyptians. But when Jesus died on the cross here it was not a quiet place either!

Except for the early morning hours, the Church of the Holy Sepulchre continues to be busy and noisy. Groups of curious tourists crowd up and down the steep stairways following their restless and talkative guides. They disturb the pilgrim who longs to meditate here.

We are on holy ground here. On this little hill just outside the walls of old Jerusalem, our good Lord died to free us from sin and death.

Let Us Pray Together

Lord Jesus Christ, we have climbed this hill of Calvary to remember your painful death for us. With the thief who hung on the cross near you, we cry out, "Jesus, remember me when you come into your kingdom" (Luke 23:42).

Perhaps here we can more clearly hear you pray just before you died, "Father, into your hands I commit my spirit" (Luke 23:45). Perhaps here, in the company of Mary and John at the foot of your cross, we can better understand your love. Maybe here we can more deeply know how precious is your blood that stained the wood of the cross, fell upon the ground and washed away our guilt. Through your wounds, O Lord, we are healed. We adore you, O Christ, and we praise you, because by your holy cross you have redeemed the world. Amen.

When We Think How Jesus Suffered

1. When we think how Je- sus suf- fered, of his love for you and me; When we stand in con- tem- pla- tion of the cross on Cal- va- ry, Then con- sid- er that the Pas- sion still con- tin- ues to this day In the sick and all who suf- fer, in the poor we turn a- way.

2. When we see Him in His dy- ing, when we hear Him call in pain, We would hur- ry to as- sure Him that it has not been in vain. But in our con- sid- er- a- tion do we tru- ly stop to hear Je- sus' bro- thers and his sis- ters who are hun- gry and so near?

3. Now the thorns were surely painful and His body cloaked in blood,
And His face was marred with spittle, and His hair was caked with mud;
But the sorrow of our Jesus can be seen by Christian eyes
In the ugly and forgotten, in the weak whom men despise.

4. When we leave the cross so lonely on that sad and sacred ground,
We must seek and find our Jesus where today he may be found;
In the clinic, in the prison, near at home or 'cross the sea,
Or wherever in deep sadness people wait to be made free.

Chapel of the Finding of the Cross

Coming down the steep stairway from Calvary visitors can turn right to walk around the ambulatory of the old Holy Sepulchre Church. There are a number of small chapels and altars to inspect. The most important and interesting of these will be found by going down still another set of steps to the ancient Chapel of St. Helena.

On the rock wall near the stairs are many small crosses. They were scratched there by the knights and squires who came here, even at the risk of death and slavery, in the twelfth century. Instead of carving their names, initials or inane mottoes as some young people of today might do, they were content to cut little crosses here near the place where the holy cross was found.

Here, the Empress Helena directed the search for the cross of Jesus in 326. This chapel commemorating its discovery is striking with its heavy Byzantine columns and dome. It now belongs to the Armenian Orthodox. The cistern that Helena had excavated contained several crosses of execution, and can be visited by going down still more stairs. It has become the Catholic Chapel of the Finding of the Cross.

We seem to be deep in the bowels of the earth. It is a stark and lonely place. A statue given by the Emperor Maximilian of Mexico honors St. Helena and her quest to find the precious relic dropped into this cistern. Tradition says that the true cross of Jesus was recognized when a sick man was cured upon touching it.

Let Us Pray Together

Lord Jesus, your saving death changed the cross from a symbol of terror and failure into our great symbol of life and victory. Here, the early Christians sought and found the very wood on which you suffered. That cross is gone, O Lord, but every cross we see and venerate today is a reminder of your love and the sign of our hope. Amen.

Behold the Cross of Jesus Christ

1. Be- hold the cross of Je -sus Christ;
2. He is our ho- ly pasch- al Lamb;

Be- hold the cross of Je- sus Christ,
He is our ho- ly pasch- al Lamb;

On which he shed his blood for us, our Lord
He proves his love for each of us, our Lord

Je- sus Christ; On which he shed his blood for
Je- sus Christ; He proves his love for each of

us, Je- sus Christ.
us, Je- sus Christ.

3. From out his heart flow streams of love;
   From out his heart flow streams of love,
   And he will wash us clean again, our Lord Jesus Christ;
   And he will wash us clean again, Jesus Christ.

4. He does not leave us orphans here;
   He does not leave us orphans here,
   But comes to make his home with us, our Lord Jesus Christ;
   But comes to make his home with us, Jesus Christ.

5. He is the way, the truth and life;
   He is the way, the truth and life,
   Who gives the peace the world can't give, our Lord Jesus Christ;
   Who gives the peace the world can't give, Jesus Christ.

6. He is the vine that gives us life;
   He is the vine that gives us life,
   And we are branches on that vine, our Lord Jesus Christ;
   And we are branches on that vine, Jesus Christ.

7. He is the shepherd of the flock;
   He is the shepherd of the flock;
   He goes and finds the sheep that's lost, our Lord Jesus Christ;
   He goes and finds the sheep that's lost, Jesus Christ.

Church of the Holy Sepulchre: The Rotunda

In spite of Hadrian's temple of Jupiter built over it, in spite of destruction ordered by the mad Caliph El Hakim in 1009, in spite of several serious fires and earthquakes, there is still something left of the tomb of Jesus. Within the Church of the Holy Sepulchre itself is a less than worthy small building called an aedicule put up in Turkish rococo style after the fire of 1808. It covers the tomb.

In front of the tomb stand large and dusty candelabra owned by the Greeks, Latins and Armenians. Each group also has thirteen lamps — plus four for the Copts — which hang above the entrance. The Christian Emperor Constantine wanted this to be the most important and beautiful shrine in the world, but it can have a melancholy aspect. The place where we honor the resurrection of Christ reflects the bad design of the nineteenth century and the scandal of a still divided Christianity.

In the late nineteenth century, the English General Charles Gordon thought it all too sad to consider the Holy Sepulchre tomb as Christ's true burial place. It did not fit his expectations and instead he found a "garden tomb" near the present Arab bus station. It looked much more like the tomb of Jesus "should" look. It really is a more pleasant place with sunshine and flowers and a picturesque old tomb. But this tomb is

Interior of the Tomb of Christ, Church of Holy Sepulchre

General Gordon's imaginative creation and certainly not the tomb of the Lord. Here in this dark rotunda is the true place, even if the centuries and architectural fashions have not been kind to it.

To see or touch the stone of the original tomb at all, it is necessary to go around to the back of the aedicule where the Copts from Egypt have a tiny chapel. A friendly monk is usually on duty there. He offers a tiny olive wood cross or holy card, a quick blessing with holy water and a chance to bend under the altar to touch the rock.

Entering the aedicule from the front, pilgrims find an anteroom with a glass-covered fragment of the round stone that sealed the tomb. There, you may then bend down to go through a low door into the sepulchral chamber. On the right was the stone bench for the body. It is now covered with a marble slab. It is here that

Catholics celebrate the Easter Mass each morning at 6:30 or 7:00. However, only five people at the most can crowd into this small chamber.

A visit to the chapel of the Syrian Christians opposite the Coptic chapel will present an authentic first-century tomb in its original condition. There can be no doubt that this area was reserved for burials. It was near the hill of execution and was just outside the walls of the city at that time. Since primitive times, it has been recognized as the tomb from which Jesus rose.

As might be expected, this Church of the Holy Sepulchre is a busy place. Armenian monks in pointed black hoods arrive off and on with vested choirboys. Franciscans direct visiting clergy who wish to celebrate Mass here. Syrians and Copts are heard chanting in languages long dead. Greek pilgrims from Cyprus or Crete are welcomed to the large area in the center of the basilica controlled by their compatriots. Nuns come through in a variety of robes and veils. Add to these the strange types which this holy city has always attracted. Some are the do-it-yourself monks in odd costumes or the vagrant holy men and women or the idiosyncratic mystics. It is all very colorful and strange. Yet in spite of everything the pilgrim knows it is truly good to be here.

If the visual distractions and conflicting sounds get to be too much, it is always possible to take refuge in the well-ordered chapel of the Franciscans to the north of the rotunda.

Let Us Pray Together

Lord Jesus Christ, for us who believe in you there can be no despair. For you have conquered sin and death. You have entered into the glory of your Father's house and have gone ahead of us to prepare a place for us too.

Your tomb before us is empty. You are not there and we are not to seek you among the dead. But this empty tomb reminds us vividly that you live and that we are called to live with you forever. Deepen our faith, O Lord. Fill us with joyful hope. And may our love for you find expression in charity for each other. Amen.

When Dawn Was Breaking

1. When dawn was break-ing came wom-en with per-fume and spi-ces. Hal-le-lu-ja! Come to a-noint Je-sus' bod-y, so hast-i-ly bur-ied. Hal-le-lu-ja!
2. "Who will roll back the great stone for us from the tomb's en-trance?" Hal-le-lu-ja! No need to wor-ry, the stone has been rolled from the en-trance. Hal-le-lu-ja!

3. Seeing a man in white garments, they bowed down in terror. Halleluja!
"Seek not the Lord among those who in death are still sleeping."
Halleluja!

4. "Jesus is risen and goes on before you in glory." Halleluja!
"Go and tell Peter and all the disciples the story." Halleluja!

5. Out of the tomb they were running to tell the disciples, Halleluja!
When without warning the Lord came and greeted them warmly.
Halleluja!

6. "Peace," Jesus said, and the women came up and did homage.
Halleluja!
"Send my disciples to Galilee where they will see me!" Halleluja!

Old Russian Easter hymn
Copyright © 1979 by Willard F. Jabusch

Garden of Gethsemane

"Gethsemane" comes from a Hebrew word which means oil press. The oil press is long gone, but olive trees of great age are still there to the east of the Old City walls beyond the Kidron valley. Near the olive trees, facing the Jericho road and the walls of Jerusalem is a large church of great dignity and solemn splendor.

A brightly colored mosaic of Christ during the agony in the garden adorns the church facade, but the dark purple alabaster windows keep the interior in constant darkness. However, it seems fitting, since this church built in 1924 covers several earlier buildings erected over the

Olive tree

rock on which Jesus is supposed to have prayed on that sorrowful night. The church has been called the Basilica of the Agony. However, many countries gave money to build it so it is called the Church of All Nations.

And the "nations" come. Japanese tourists with the inevitable cameras, earnest Germans with heavy guidebooks. There are Texas pentecostals who kneel, hold hands, weep and pray on the garden path outside the church. And there are Italians with their village priests buying olive-wood rosaries.

Beneath the branches of old olive trees here Jesus experienced great desolation and entered into a profound prayer of trust and obedience. Here was the place of betrayal by a friend and apostle. Here the hands of the Son of God were tied by rough soldiers and he was led away under arrest (Mark 14: 26-52).

Let Us Pray Together

Lord Jesus, here you were held in the grip of a terrible fear. Here in the Garden of Gethsemane, the dread and loneliness were so great that the Gospel says you sweated blood. Here you longed for human companionship but your apostles only fell asleep. They did not realize how much you needed them. You knew that you could have escaped from this place and from the torture and death of the next day. A brisk walk up the path would have taken you around to Bethany and onto the open hills of Judea and to safety beyond the Jordan. But then, we would not have been healed by your wounds. Lord, be with us in our own anxieties. Stay near us when our hearts are heavy. Amen.

Jesus Went With His Disciples

1. Je- sus went with his dis- ci- ples
2. When He came, all his dis- ci- ples

to a gar- den where he prayed;
out of grief were fast a- sleep;

Dark the trees, lone- ly that gar- den;
Je- sus said: Why are you sleep- ing?

on His knees He fell and prayed.
Rise and pray you do not fall.

1-4: Fa- ther, if you would, take this cup from me,

Yet not mine, but your will be done,

Yet not mine, but your will be done.

3. Simon, are your eyes so heavy that you've fallen fast asleep;
   For the spirit is so willing, but the flesh is, oh, so weak.

4. Now the time for sleep has ended, now the moment is at hand,
   For the Son of Man is given to the hands of sinful men.

Traditional Polish and Lithuanian
Copyright © 1978 by Willard F. Jabusch

Saint Peter
"in Gallicantu"

A strange Latin name was given to this modern church to the south of the Old City. In English it would be called "the Church of St. Peter at the Crowing of the Cock." Under this church are a series of cellars and cisterns cut out of the rock. It is quite possible that they were once used as a prison, rather like Rome's fearful Mamertine Prison where luckless prisoners were let down into the darkness by a rope. But it is not likely that Jesus was kept a prisoner at this site. Nor is it likely that these ancient cellars formed part of the house of the high priest Caiaphas, as was once claimed.

But next to the church there is a wonderful set of stone steps that led from Siloam and the valley up to Mount Sion. It certainly dates from Roman times and it most probably was used by Jesus, Mary and the Apostles. Here is commemorated the denial of Christ by Peter (Mark 14: 66-72) and the place where "he went out and wept bitterly" (Matthew 26: 75).

Let Us Pray Together

Lord, all of the frightened apostles fled and hid themselves somewhere in the city. None insisted on following you and standing at your side. But only Peter swore three times that he never knew you. Yet, Lord, you saw something good in him. His tears went beyond mere shame and remorse to honest contrition and renewed love.

Did he sit on one of these very steps and resolve to follow you again? Was it seeing you led up this long stairway that made him regret his betrayal?

Lord, look also into our eyes. Call us to penance and conversion. Forgive us and use us in your service as you did the humbled Peter. Amen.

Lord, I Have Often Betrayed You

Refrain

Lord, I have oft- en be- trayed you,
So man- y times gone a- stray;
Still you con- tin- ue to love me,
With me each step of the way.

Verses

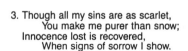

1. Pe- ter de- nied You that eve- ning;
2. Pe- ter went out and was weep- ing,

There in the court- yard he swore,
Bit- ter the tears for his crime;

Three times de- ny- ing he knew You,
When a heart cries in con- tri- tion,

Just as You warned him be- fore.
Bless- ed the place and the time.

3. Though all my sins are as scarlet,
    You make me purer than snow;
Innocence lost is recovered,
    When signs of sorrow I show.

Asturian melody
Copyright © 1979 by Willard F. Jabusch

The Cenacle

For many years Christian pilgrims were not even allowed to enter the Cenacle or the "Upper Room" of the Last Supper. The building was much reconstructed by the Franciscans in the fourteenth century and has a definite Gothic style. But later it became Moslem property. A tomb on the first floor was venerated as that of King David. The whole building was declared off-limits for Christians.

Now things have changed. Yet the Cenacle remains empty except for the reminders of its Islamic use for many centuries. The Holy Eucharist is not celebrated in this central shrine of the Eucharist.

The Cenacle room can seem barren and dark. A huge stone construction built in 1928 cuts off some light. It indicated the direction of Mecca when Moslems worshipped here. There is no place to sit except on some stone stairs or on a platform. Nevertheless, this is a room of great atmosphere. If you are fortunate enough to be undisturbed, this place can easily lead you to prayer. Take out a pocket New Testament here and slowly read the Last Supper discourse in John's Gospel (John 13-18). Picture Jesus washing the feet of his apostles and then joining with them in the Passover supper. See Judas leaving the table and disappearing down the stairs. Watch the Lord taking the bread and the wine, blessing them and giving his friends the farewell gift of himself. Hear Jesus and the eleven remaining apostles sing the final psalm before they leave Mount Sion and walk down through the valley of Kidron to the olive grove of Gethsemane.

Cenacle or Upper Room interior

Providing there are no verbose guides herding their weary charges in and out, it is not difficult here to relive the events, to hear again the voices of that farewell supper. Tradition has it that this upper chamber was twice blest. It is said that the apostles later gathered here with Mary on the first Pentecost and received the gift of the Holy Spirit.

Perhaps the emptiness of this Upper Room is a blessing. Bare of pictures, statues, candles and pews, it is a space to be filled with memories. It is quite empty except for the prayers of the faithful.

On the ground floor of this rambling building below the Cenacle is a room containing a large cenotaph or stone tomb memorial covered in brocade. Since 1967, it has become a popular Jewish shrine since it is said to be the tomb of David. However, there is no record of it before the twelfth century after Christ. (The Cenacle on the upper floor of the building is attested since the fifth century.) Visitors are encouraged to light candles and receive a Hebrew blessing in ante-rooms of the shrine. But expect to pay!

A small garden leads to the "Cellar of the Holocaust." It is a series of dark rooms dedicated to the memory of the millions who died under Hitler. Many Hebrew inscriptions on the walls record names of murdered relatives and friends. Terrible scenes photographed by Nazi guards show an agony which took place in our own century. It is salutary that we be reminded of all of this so close to the Upper Room. We must remember what is possible when "Christians" forget what Jesus said there.

Let Us Pray Together

Lord Jesus, in this Upper Room on Mount Sion, we think of the mystery of the Holy Eucharist. This was your own Body and Blood given to us as nourishment for our life journey. We hear again your words from the Upper Room which command us to serve one another in love and unity.

May the Spirit fill us, as Mary and the apostles were filled here. We pray for the courage and zeal to go from this room into a world divided by selfishness and hatred. Help us also to overcome our fears that we may also be messengers of forgiveness, reunion and peace. Amen.

Come to His Table

Verses

1. The Lord at the sup- per the night be- fore he died Took bread, blest and broke it, and gave it to his friends, took bread, blest and broke it, and gave it to his friends.

2. The Lord showed com- pas- sion, the Lord has proved his love; He gives us his Bod- y that all of us be one, He gives us his Bod- y that all of us be one.

Refrain

So come to His ta- ble, His sup- per brings de- light; Why stand out- side hun- gry and lone- ly in the night? Why stand out- side hun- gry and lone- ly in the night?

3. He took from the table the cup of wine and said,
"Now take this and drink from the chalice of my Blood,
Now take this and drink from the chalice of my Blood."

Mexican hymn
Copyright © 1978 by Willard F. Jabusch

Dormition Abbey

In 1898, the German Kaiser William II bought land on Mount Sion. He had already built the fine new Church of the Redeemer close to the Holy Sepulchre for his Evangelical Lutheran subjects. This new property included the site of a Church of Our Lady of Mount Sion built by the Crusaders and demolished in 1219 by the Arabs. Here, to please his Catholic subjects from Bavaria and the Rhineland, the Kaiser commissioned a great Basilica of the Dormition (or the "Falling Asleep of Our Lady"). The resulting

Basilica of the Dormition, Mount Sion

complex of buildings includes a notable bell tower and a monastery for German Benedictine monks.

The generosity of pilgrims has provided for impressive mosaics in the elegant domed church and a series of interesting statues and altars in the crypt. There is a lovely statue of the Virgin in the repose of death and one of ivory and ebony presented by the President of the Ivory Coast. Recently, a splendid pipe organ has been installed. Catholic pilgrim groups from Germany and Austria tend to gather here for their liturgies, but anyone is welcome to join the Benedictine community for the monastic Office of psalms and prayers. The high abbey church with its bell tower has become the principal landmark on Mount Sion and the most important Marian shrine in the city. Repairs to the stonework are now underway and it is fascinating to watch the Arab stonecutters chipping away in the lane outside the church. Their resources are those of the medieval masons: chisels, hammers and lots of patient hard work.

Let Us Pray Together

Dear Jesus, we do not know when your mother's earthly life was over and when she "fell asleep" in the peace of God. Were the Apostles gathered around her deathbed? Did she have some last words for them? Surely you welcomed her with love to her eternal home.

Someday we too must leave this earthly Jerusalem for the heavenly Jerusalem, O Lord. Trusting in God's love and forgiveness, may we peacefully fall asleep in death to awaken to everlasting life with you, Mary, Joseph, the apostles and all the saints. May the pilgrimage of our life through this world lead us always to our true home with you. Amen.

How Could the World

1. How could the world con- tain her, the
   To heav- en she's as- cend- ed to
2. Our hearts are made for heav- en, yet
   We some- times turn from Je- sus, his

moth- er of our God?
be the an- gels' queen.
e- vil they may choose;
bless- ings we re- fuse.

1. Yet such is her com- pas- sion, her
2. So Mar- y, in your good- ness, to

kind- ness for us all, she
us a moth- er be; From

al- ways is a moth- er on
self- ish ness and ha- tred, oh

whom we still can call.
pray that we be free!

3. As Jesus is our Brother, who shows us how to live,
So Mary is our mother with hope and love to give;
In sickness, war, and worry, then Mary, be close by!
You hear the sick folk praying, the captive's lonely cry.

4. The sailor calls upon you when far away from home,
To lead him to safe harbor, from wind and ocean's foam;
The dying see your image and speak your gentle name;
To help us go to Jesus has always been your aim.

Pool of Siloam and Hezekiah's Tunnel

Even by modern standards this tunnel due south of the Old City must be considered a major feat of engineering. King Hezekiah (727-698 B.C.) had it cut through the rock to prevent Sennacherib, King of Assyria, from gaining control of the water supply when he attacked Jerusalem. "Why," they said, "should the kings of Assyria find plenty of water when they arrive?" (2 Chronicles 32: 4).

The spring of Gihon ("gushing") had flowed out into the Kidron valley. Its source was camouflaged and two of Hezekiah's teams began cutting through the rock. One cut from the spring, the other from the Pool of Siloam. The Bible says that Hezekiah "constructed the pool and the conduit to bring water into the city" (2 Kings 20: 20). "It was Hezekiah who stopped the upper outlet of the waters of Gihon and directed them down to the west side of the Citadel of David" (2 Chronicles 32:30).

An inscription in archaic Hebrew script was found inside the tunnel long afterwards. It recorded the exciting day when Hezekiah's men broke through. "...the miners struck, one against the other, pick against pick, and the water flowed from the spring towards the pool, 1200 cubits. The height of the rock above the head of the miners was 100 cubits." The inscription was cut out of the tunnel by the Turks and can now be seen in the Istanbul Museum.

Today it is possible to wade from the spring through this historic tunnel to the Pool of Si-

Pool of Siloam

loam. The water rises above the waist and your candle must be held high. Bits of sharp stone can be a problem for bare feet. Not a recommended adventure for the hesitant or claustrophobic!

But the Pool of Siloam is really famous because of Jesus' cure there of the man born blind (John 9). The pool can more easily be reached from the road and down a flight of steps. Some friendly young Arabs will be there to watch your car, sell you olive-wood items and guide you down to the water level. Fragments from the colonnade now lie in the water that was long considered to have curative powers.

The church built above the pool was destroyed by the Persians in 614. A mosque was built here in the 1890s.

Let Us Pray Together

Lord Jesus, you told the man born blind, "Go, wash in the Pool of Siloam." The man went and washed and came home seeing. We have come here today with our blindness. Cure us too, O Lord, for we also want to come home seeing. Seeing what is really important and good in life. Seeing more clearly the way we should follow you. Seeing you.

The man you cured here said, "Lord, I believe." And he worshipped you. May we do the same. Amen.

God Loved the World So Dearly

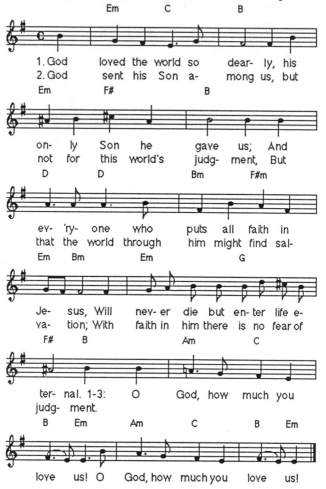

3. The Light has come among us, but men preferred the darkness;
The evil hate the light for all it's showing,
But good folk come to see their God more clearly.
O God, how much you love us! O God, how much you love us!

Italian hymn
Copyright © 1979 by Willard F. Jabusch

The Church of St. Anne

Use as an Islamic school certainly saved the Church of St. Anne near St. Stephen's Gate. The widow of the first Crusader king of Jerusalem had it built in 1142 on the site where Joachim and Anne, Mary's parents, reportedly lived. Napoleon III received it much later as a gift from the Ottoman Sultan in 1856. It has belonged to the French government ever since.

The austere whiteness of St. Anne's Church matches the robes of the "White Fathers of Africa." They are French missionary priests who care for this church and the adjacent seminary. The architecture is severe, almost unornamented Romanesque from the twelfth century. It is noble and beautiful; there is probably no church in the

Church of St. Anne

Holy Land better suited for the contemporary liturgy. The acoustics are superb; a hymn sung by even a small group will sound like the work of a mighty choir.

A staircase leads down to a simple chapel of the Blessed Sacrament where pilgrims can see a graceful old wooden statue of the Virgin. St. Anne's may be the most serene place in Jerusalem.

Let Us Pray Together

O God, you inspire the minds and imaginations of men and women to create what is beautiful and good. This Church of St. Anne has survived as an example of simple beauty, strength and grace. Once again it is a place for Christian worship and a wondrous setting for singing the praise of Jesus and his saints. May it be a welcoming house of prayer for men and women of many countries and many faiths. With sincere and humble words may each of us speak to you and find in your will our joy and peace. Amen.

Song of Good News

1. O- pen your ears, Oh Chris-tian peo- ple,
2. They who have ears to hear His mes- sage,

O- pen your ears and hear good news!
They who have ears, then let them hear!

O- pen your hearts, Oh roy- al priest- hood,
They who would learn the way of wis- dom

God has come to you. God has spo- ken
let them hear God's word.

to His peo- ple, Hal- le- lu- jah!

And His words are words of wis- dom,

Hal- le- lu- jah! God has spo- ken

to His peo- ple Hal- le- lu- jah!

And His words are words of wis-dom,

Hal- le- lu- jah!

3. Israel comes to greet the Savior; Judah is glad to see His day!
From East and West the peoples travel, He will show the way.

Israeli folksong
Copyright © 1966, 1984 by Willard F. Jabusch

Jerusalem / 77

The Pool of Bethesda

Just to the side of the Church of St. Anne is an area that has been extensively excavated. This was the famous Pool of Bethesda where Jesus performed one of the sabbath cures that so angered the super-pious of Jerusalem (John 5: 1-9).

Since this pool was near the Sheep Gate it was called in Latin "piscina porbatica" (sheep pool). It was considered to have healing properties. The man who was crippled for thirty-eight years was one of many sick who came here in Jesus' time. By the second century, there was even a shrine here to Asclepius, the Greek god of healing. There are also the ruins of a fifth-century Byzantine basilica and of a Crusader chapel above the dried-out pool.

The whole site looks rather barren and confusing today. But there can be no doubt that this was the place described in the Gospel. Perhaps pilgrims can use their imagination to rebuild the porches around the pool and see again the crippled man and the compassionate Jesus.

Let Us Pray Together

Lord Jesus, you came down from Galilee for the feast and had pity on a crippled man here at the Pool of Bethesda. You said to him, "Rise, take up your bed and walk."

We too are crippled, Lord. Crippled by our fears, crippled by memories of our sins and failures, crippled by sadness and despair. We have waited so long to be cured, but we cannot achieve it by ourselves. We need to hear you tell us, "Rise and walk." With your grace we will do so. Amen.

Down by the Pool of Bethesda

Capo 3: Em

1. Down by the pool of Beth- es- da,
2. When Je- sus saw him, he asked him,

Gath- ered the sick and blind and lame.
"Friend, do you want to walk a- gain?"

One man had been so long crip- pled,
"Sir, I have no one to help me

Thir- ty- eight sad years he could not walk.
Down to the pool's wat- er when it stirs."

3. "Rise to your feet," Jesus answered;
      "Take up your bed and walk again!"
   Standing, he took up his stretcher;
      Step by step he walked before the crowd.

4. Lord, we have also been crippled,
      Crippled by ignorance and shame,
   Wasting our years and our talents,
      Waiting without strength to rise and move.

5. This is the day of our healing;
      Lord, come to us and help us stand;
   Come as you did at Bethesda;
      Speak to us, Lord; tell us, "Rise and walk!"

Ukrainian hymn
Copyright © 1979 by Willard F. Jabusch

The Way of
the Cross
(Via Dolorosa)

I remember that it was Father Benoit, the great French Dominican biblical scholar, who gently but firmly broke the news to us: The best scholarship today indicates that Jesus was condemned by Pilate in the Citadel near the Jaffa Gate.

Therefore, the "Way of the Cross," the "Via Dolorosa," should begin there and not at the Antonia Fortress where medieval tradition placed the first of the stations of the cross.

It is unlikely, however, that anyone really wants to establish a new "via crucis" or "way of the cross." It would have to be followed from the Citadel (now a museum), down the steps of crowded David Street and then left to the Holy Sepulchre. The traditional path may not be historically authentic but it has been followed by thousands of pilgrims for hundreds of years. It is a path of prayer worth following with humility and devotion. Its chapels make it easier to pause and think about our suffering Jesus than the busy bazaar of David Street.

(Following each station, sing one verse of the song WHATSOEVER YOU DO, found on pages 102-103.)

FIRST STATION:

Jesus Is Condemned to Death

A good place to begin is in the garden of the Monastery of the Flagellation, about a city block up from St. Stephen's Gate and past the church of St. Anne. You will find the entrance on your right. There are two chapels and a cloister walk.

Cloister walk at the Monastery of the Flagellation, 1st Station

Let Us Pray Together

Lord Jesus, innocent of all sin, you were condemned by those who considered your death expedient or "useful." May our decisions and our lives be guided, O Lord, by what is just and good not merely by what is convenient and popular. May the words of your Gospel and the example of your life form our consciences. Amen.

(Sing verse one of WHATSOEVER YOU DO found on pages 102-103.)

SECOND STATION:

Jesus Takes Up His Cross

For the second station, you can go into the beautiful chapel of the Convent of the Sisters of Sion on the right, although a station marker is fixed outside. Forming part of the sanctuary of the chapel is an authentic Roman archway. In the basement is the great stone pavement, the "Lithostrotos," of the Antonia Fortress on which the soldiers scratched the markings for games to pass the time.

Let Us Pray Together

Jesus, our brother, the wooden crosspiece was placed on your shoulders here. You stooped under the weight of the wood and of the guilt and suffering of humankind. When a cross we did not choose comes into our lives, may we think of you. For you will surely think of us and understand our pain. Amen.

(Sing verse two of WHATSOEVER YOU DO found on pages 102-103.)

THIRD STATION:

Jesus Falls the First Time

Shopkeepers along the Via Dolorosa are not bashful about seeking customers, even among pilgrims trying to follow Christ's steps. But it is at the end of the street, after the left turn for the third station, that commercial activity becomes more intense. If the Armenian Catholic Church is open, you may seek refuge there to pray this station. Otherwise, a station marker outside provides a stone carving of the fallen Christ above the chapel door.

Let Us Pray Together

Jesus, Man of Sorrows, acquainted with infirmity, be with us. Help us in our times of moral, emotional, or physical weakness. Spiritual directors, physicians and psychologists may all be of help but only you truly understand our infirmities. Only you can really be one with us in our weakness. Amen.

(Sing verse three of WHATSOEVER YOU DO found on pages 102-103.)

FOURTH STATION:
Jesus Meets His Sorrowing Mother

Did Mary look rather like one of the Arab women of today? They still keep a traditional dress and a rural simplicity when they come in from the desert to the streets of the Old City.

We stop on this crowded street full of noisy children, an occasional donkey and weary tourists to remember the painful meeting of mother and son. Like the third, the fourth station presents pilgrims on this route with a stone sculpture for meditation. A half bust of Christ and his mother is set above an oratory door facing the street.

Let Us Pray Together

Jesus, did you see your mother's face in the crowd? Did your eyes meet for a moment? She wanted so to help you but she could not.

How many parents today have no food to give a starving child and no medicine for a sick baby? And how many are helpless to stop the murder of a son or daughter by a "death squad" or by the violence of gang warfare? Comfort them, O Lord Jesus. Comfort your poor people. Amen.

(Sing verse four of WHATSOEVER YOU DO found on pages 102-103.)

Stone sculpture of Mary meeting Jesus,
4th Station

FIFTH STATION:

Simon Helps Jesus With His Cross

We are not used to praying in the streets and we may feel awkward stopping at this corner in order to pray the fifth station. Here, the Via Dolorosa turns to the right. Too many distractions. Too dirty. Too noisy. But we must pause to remember Simon the Cyrenean who was made to carry the crossbeam behind Jesus in just such a common street.

Let Us Pray Together

Jesus, a reluctant Simon found the crossbeam put upon his own shoulders here. Help us, O Lord, to lift with somewhat greater enthusiasm the burdens from your brothers and sisters. In doing so we show our love for you. Give us the faith we need to recognize you in those despised by the world. Amen.

(Sing verse five of WHATSOEVER YOU DO found on pages 102-103.)

SIXTH STATION:

Veronica Wipes the Face of Jesus

Climbing the steps of the Via Dolorosa we discover the sixth station marker in the wall to the left. On the left as well is a simple chapel for pilgrims maintained by the Little Sisters of Jesus. They are members of a modern contemplative order who live in great poverty and simplicity in some of the most remote places in the world. They have a little shop next to the humble and beautiful chapel; they make and sell reproductions of old icons. If the street entrance to the chapel is locked it is possible to enter through the shop.

Let Us Pray Together

Lord, we know Veronica was not mentioned in the Gospels. But somehow it seems right that someone would have dared to step out from the crowd to do for you a simple act of kindness. May we know you, Lord, when your face is marred by the blood, sweat, dust and spittle of the passion. May we also know you in the faces of the aged, the young, the poor, the sick and the oppressed. Amen.

(Sing verse six of WHATSOEVER YOU DO found on pages 102-103.)

SEVENTH STATION:

Jesus Falls the Second Time

Lights, smells, colors, crowds. All is movement here for we now turn into a major bazaar, a street both narrow and intensely animated. It is the Arab suq or market and it is easy to miss the seventh station. But pause at this corner to consider Jesus falling again amid the pushing and angry crowd.

Let Us Pray Together

Jesus, fallen in the dirt of the street, exhausted and weak, is there no one to reach out to you? Is there no one to help you to your feet? Help us now, O Lord, to lift up those who are discouraged by many falls. Help us to reach out to those who are despondent and weary, or close to despair. For you have suffered all of this to bring us hope. Lord, you have fallen in the crowded street that we might rise to new life. Amen.

(Sing verse seven of WHATSOEVER YOU DO found on pages 102-103.)

Street scene along Via Dolorosa

EIGHTH STATION:

Jesus Meets the Women of Jerusalem

To find the eighth station, go up Aquabat el Khanqa, a street ascending to the west. Look for a stone cross on the wall of an Orthodox church there. If you can't find it, don't be upset. Almost any place will provide a setting for you to think of Jesus turning to the women who were lamenting his fate. "Daughters of Jerusalem," you can hear him say, "do not weep for me; weep rather for yourselves and for your children" (Luke 23:28).

Stone cross, 8th Station

Let Us Pray Together

Lord Jesus, you do not ask for pity and tears. You do not require an emotional sympathy. Rather, you ask for justice, conversion of life, love of our enemies, purity of heart, humble service to those who are neither beautiful nor charming. Following you and carrying the cross is not easy for us, Lord. Speak to us on the way. Amen.

(Sing verse eight of WHATSOEVER YOU DO found on pages 102-103.)

NINTH STATION:

Jesus Falls the Third Time

For this ninth station, go back to the extension of the street called "Sug Khan ez-Zeit." Turn right and follow it to a staircase. The ninth station is marked above by an old pillar. If you are older and getting a bit hot and weary, there is nothing to prevent you from praying this station at the foot of the twenty-eight steps.

Let Us Pray Together

Lord, if the Cyrenean was still carrying your cross, is it possible you fell this time from a heaviness of heart? Did you foresee the horrors that would be committed, even by those who would call themselves your followers?

We who live in this century of horrors also have a terrible heaviness of heart. There have been too many atrocities, firebombings, atom bombings, death camps and labor battalions. We have seen too much of injustice, prejudice, abortions, assassinations, dictatorships of the left and the right. We feel pulled down by the weight of the world's evils and by our helplessness. Come, Lord, and save us from hopelessness. Amen.

(Sing verse nine of WHATSOEVER YOU DO found on pages 102-103.)

Jesus Is Stripped of His Garments

Come back down the stairs to follow the Via Dolorosa to the next, the tenth station. Continue around to the right and go into the courtyard of the Basilica of the Holy Sepulchre. The remaining five stations are inside. The hill of Calvary is to your right inside the church. An outside stairway which once led up to a chapel and entrance there, is now closed. The Crusaders once used it to reach Calvary. Now pilgrims must first enter the church and then climb another set of stairs. The tenth station may be prayed either outside or inside the Basilica.

Let Us Pray Together

Good Jesus, rough hands pulled away your clothes and left you naked before the mob. Help us, in this shameless age, to understand your shame. Let us not, O Lord, become accustomed to pornography, the exploitation and abuse of women and children, and to the corruption of the innocent. May purity and holiness be once again esteemed and desired. For we know, dear Jesus, that we find happiness not in lust and self-indulgence, but in following you. Amen.

(Sing verse 10 of WHATSOEVER YOU DO found on pages 102-103.)

Jesus Is Nailed to the Cross

For the eleventh station, pilgrims climb the stairs to the chapel and altar on the right. This Latin domain features a large mosaic that depicts Jesus being nailed to the cross. Beneath the floor is the rock of Calvary.

Large mosaic of Jesus being nailed to cross, 11th Station

Let Us Pray Together

Jesus, how much you suffered for us! How painful the nails were that held you to the cross! How great the agony when the cross was lifted up on this hill of execution. We cannot come here and remember what happened and why it happened without examining our own lives. We remember your crucifixion here and acknowledge our mediocrity and selfishness. Lord, may we be deeply moved by the example of your love. Amen.

(Sing verse 11 of WHATSOEVER YOU DO found on pages 102-103.)

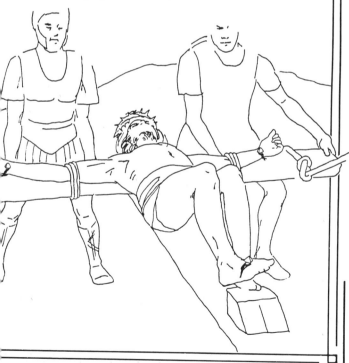

TWELFTH STATION:

Jesus Dies on the Cross

On the left side of Calvary is the Greek Orthodox altar of the crucifixion and the twelfth station. Here the pilgrim comes to pray and consider the saving death of Jesus Christ who was both God and man. A place below the altar exposes the place where the Savior's cross was wedged into rock. "A man can have no greater love than to lay down his life for his friends" (John 15: 13).

Let Us Pray Together

Jesus, we see you dying on the cross and we want to thank you for the love which you have for each of us. It is a love so strong and so tender, a love which is the cause of our hope. Through your death we are offered life, "by your holy cross you have redeemed the world." May we never cease trusting in the mystery of your redemptive sacrifice and the certainty of your never-ending love. Amen.

(Sing verse 12 of WHATSOEVER YOU DO found on pages 102-103.)

Jesus Is Taken Down From the Cross

There is a small altar with a Portuguese statue of the Sorrowful Mother between the eleventh and twelfth stations. This is the designated thirteenth station. Some people, however, prefer to pray the thirteenth station by going back down the stairs to the so-called "Stone of Anointing" near the Basilica entrance. It is a large stone slab of fairly recent origin which recalls the preparation of Jesus' body for burial.

Let Us Pray Together

Jesus, Joseph of Arimathea and Nicodemus took your body down from the cross, but it was your mother who received it into her arms. Be with all those who must stand by the bodies of their loved ones. Console them in their sorrow and give them hope in eternal life. Your followers, even your own dear mother, are not held immune from pain and loss. But we do not mourn as those who have no hope. Be close to us, Lord, at the time of death. Amen.

(Sing verse 13 of WHATSOEVER YOU DO found on pages 102-103.)

FOURTEENTH STATION:

Jesus Is Laid in the Tomb

We now enter the great rotunda built over the Sepulchre of the Lord. This is the last, the fourteenth station of the cross on this Via Dolorosa. Almost all of the original cave has been cut away. It has been replaced with a small building of Turkish design. Here we pray the last of the stations of the cross.

Let Us Pray Together

Lord Jesus, we have been privileged to follow the "Way of the Cross" and contemplate your path of humiliation and pain on that first Good Friday. But here where your body was placed in the tomb, we think of your resurrection and your victory over sin and death. May we never forget that we follow you, the Lord of light. You overcome the darkness of evil and give us a share in divine life and a foretaste of heaven. Amen.

(Sing verse 14 of WHATSOEVER YOU DO found on pages 102-103.)

Exterior of Tomb of Christ, 14th Station

Whatsoever You Do

Refrain

What- so- ev- er you do to the
least of my peo- ple, that you
do un- to me.

Verses

1. When I was hun- gry, you
2. When I was home- less, you

gave me to eat; When I was
o- pened your door; When I was

thirs- ty, you gave me to drink.
na- ked, you gave me your coat.

Now en- ter in- to the home of my Fa-

ther.

3. When I was weary, you helped me find rest;
    When I was anxious, you calmed all my fears.
   Now enter into the home of my Father.

4. When I was little, you taught me to read;
    When I was lonely, you gave me your love.
   Now enter into the home of my Father.

5. Mocked for my language, my customs, my race,
    You dared to help me, you carried my cross.
   Now enter into the home of my Father.

6. You saw me covered with spittle and blood;
    You knew my features, though grimy with sweat.
   Now enter into the home of my Father.

7. In a strange country, you made me at home;
    Seeking employment, you found me a job.
   Now enter into the home of my Father.

8. When I was aged, you bothered to smile;
    When I was restless, you listened and cared.
   Now enter into the home of my Father.

9. When in a prison, you came to my cell;
    When I had fallen, you helped me get up.
   Now enter into the home of my Father.

10. Stripped of all dignity, shamed and afraid,
     You felt my anguish and stayed by my side.
    Now enter into the home of my Father.

11. Stretched on a sickbed, you cared for my needs;
     Frightened and hurting, I welcomed your voice.
    Now enter into the home of my Father.

12. When I was kidnapped, then tortured and killed,
     You took the risk to speak out for the poor.
    Now enter into the home of my Father.

13. You knew the value of each human life;
     You fought to save me from those who destroy.
    Now enter into the home of my Father.

14. You brought me comfort when I was bereaved;
     You sensed how deep was my loss and my pain.
    Now enter into the home of my Father.

15. You helped my little ones rise up and live;
     Share in my victory, share in my joy!
    Now enter into the home of my Father.

"Dominus Flevit" Chapel

Without a doubt, following the Via Dolorosa is among every Christian pilgrim's most treasured memories. But the Holy City holds many other blessings. Guests at the Inter-Continental Hotel to the west of the Old City enjoy one of the great panoramas of the world. All Jerusalem is spread out before them to the north and west. At sunset, the domes, spires, roofs of the tightly clustered houses of the Old City and its great walls all take on a wondrous warmth and majesty. Buses pull up below the hotel, and the tourists spill out and some have themselves photographed on a reluctant camel. Too bad that more do not take the path down to the right to a small chapel with a Latin name and a distinctive silhouette.

This chapel was built only in 1955, but on fifth-century foundations. There is an old mosaic inscription here, but the most beautiful feature is a large window above the altar with the outline of a chalice. Here the wonder of the view from the "Dominus Flevit" ("The Lord Wept") Chapel becomes more focused. Here tradition says that Jesus himself looked across at the golden city and reproached it for its indifference and hardness of heart. In fact, he was so moved by love and hurt by rejection that the Lord wept (Matthew 23:37, Luke 19:41-44).

View of Jerusalem from "Dominus Flevit" chapel

Let Us Pray Together

Lord, how you loved your people and desired to gather them close to you "as a hen gathers her chicks under her wings." But it was not to be. May we never reject you and your Gospel message, O Lord. Let us rather respond with joy and enthusiasm. Amen.

O Jerusalem

1. Sil- ver and gold in the late set- ting sun are the roof- tops and walls of the cit- y; Splen- did to see in the soft dy- ing light are the tem- ple and domes of the cit- y. Bur- nished with gold yet bur- dened with pain, O Je-

2. Just as the hen likes to gath- er her brood, so would Je- sus have gath- ered your chil- dren, But you would not hear the word of your Lord, hear the word that would bring you sal- va- tion. Cit- y of pro- phets, cit- y of kings, do you

ru- sa- lem, roy- al cit- y,
see your Mes- si- ah weep- ing?

Bur- nished with gold yet
Cit- y of pro- phets,

bur- dened with pain, O Je-
cit- y of kings, do you

ru- sa- lem, roy- al cit- y.
see your Mes- si- ah weep- ing?

3. Set on a hill for the nations to see,
    soon your pride will be turned into ashes;
   City that silenced the brave prophets' voice,
    soon your temple will be desolation.
   City of God yet city of men,
    if you knew how your Savior loved you!
   City of God yet city of men,
    if you knew how your Savior loved you!

4. Proud was the pilgrim who marched through your gate,
    through the porch of the bright marble temple;
   Happy the man who could dwell in your walls,
    in the crown of the lion of Judah.
   Boast not of David, Solomon's gold –
    Jesus came and you did not know him;
   Boast not of David, Solomon's gold –
    Jesus came and you did not know him.

Finnish melody
Copyright © 1976, 1986 by Willard F. Jabusch

Church of the "Pater Noster"

In early Christian times, a great church stood at this site built over a cave. It was linked to the mystery of the Ascension of Our Lord. Since it was located on the Mount of Olives, it was called Eleona ("of olives").

When the Ascension of Jesus was later commemorated further up the hill, this beautiful church and the cave under the sanctuary became the place to remember the teaching of Jesus. There is a record from the year 384 stating that portions (verses 1-26) of Matthew's twenty-fourth chapter were read here on the Tuesday of Holy Week. Later, it became the place to honor Jesus teaching the "Our Father" to the Apostles.

In the twelfth century, marble plaques with the prayer in Hebrew, Greek and Latin could be seen. Today tiled panels present the "Lord's Prayer" in eighty languages. A French noblewoman bought the property in 1868 and founded a Carmelite convent behind the half-reconstructed church.

This is not a heavily visited shrine; therefore, it is a good place for quiet prayer under the trees or in the cloister-walk. It is a special place to pray slowly and peacefully the "Our Father" (Luke 11: 2-4).

Let Us Pray Together

Lord, teach us to pray! Help us to find the words to express what is in our hearts, the praise and thanksgiving, the sorrow for our sins and the deep need we have for your help. We have experienced enough in our lives to know we cannot make it on our own. We reach out to you; we want to speak sincerely and honestly.

Lord teach us to pray as you taught your disciples:

Our Father who art in heaven
hallowed be thy name;
thy kingdom come, thy will be done
on earth as it is in heaven.
Give us this day our daily bread;
and forgive us our trespasses
as we forgive those who trespass against us;
and lead us not into temptation
but deliver us from evil.

Teach Us, Lord

1. Teach us, Lord, the ways of pray- ing; ev- 'ry word we'll be o- bey- ing; Tell us what we should be say- ing to our Fa- ther great and good.

2. In your name we go be- fore Him; sing- ing prais- es we a- dore him; Trust- ing all we need He'll give us when we ask in Je- sus name.

3. Daily bread our God will give us; all our sins with joy forgive us;
   Send to us the Holy Spirit, bringing courage, peace and love.

4. Jesus' name we'll go on saying, every day as we are praying,
   For we know the Father hears us when we speak our brother's name.

5. Come, good folk of every nation, if you too would find salvation;
   Know that God, your loving Father, hears you when you pause to pray.

German melody
Copyright © 1977 by Willard F. Jabusch

Ascension Mosque

Luke is the only evangelist to mention the Ascension of Jesus, but he did not precisely locate the place (Luke 24: 50-52). In his second work, the Acts of the Apostles, he placed the Ascension site somewhere on the Mount of Olives (Acts 1: 6-12). More than a historical event, this was a dramatic way of marking the end of the earthly mission of Jesus and the start of the missionary work of his followers. Early Christians celebrated the Ascension feast at the cave in what is now the Church of the "Pater Noster."

Ascension Mosque

In 384, the pilgrim Egeria said the liturgy celebrating the event took place on a nearby hill in the open air. The Crusaders later built the octagon shrine which we see now, but it was open to the sky. It was a rather lovely architectural sign of the Ascension. But the Moslem Saladin gave the building to his followers in 1198. They added a roof and made it into a mosque. It remains Moslem property today. It has a dingy and desolate quality. Some pilgrims believe that it has been turned into a money-making enterprise by some young locals. A wise old Arab offers camel rides on the road outside.

Let Us Pray Together

Lord Jesus, we must continue your work among the people of our time and our place. It is our task as your followers to see that the Good News is preached to the poor. We must see to it that the sick are cared for, that the oppressed are made free. We thank you for being called to take part in your holy work, and we ask for your constant help and encouragement.

We cannot now see you walking and teaching on the hillsides of Palestine or in the streets of Jerusalem. But let us come to discover you in the least of your brothers and sisters all around us. Amen.

Jesus Sent Forth His Disciples

1. Je- sus sent forth his dis-
2. Go and preach these words of

ci- ples well in- struct- ed for the
wis- dom, that the King- dom is ap-

jour- ney: For your trip take noth- ing
proach- ing; Cure the sick and cleanse the

with you, walk- ing stick or food or
lep- ers, raise the dead and drive out

mon- ey.
de- mons.

3. When you go into a dwelling, "Peace be with you" is your greeting.
   Be as cautious as a serpent, but like doves be ever gentle.

4. They will bring you for a trial with their kings and with their rulers;
   Do not worry, words are given from the Spirit of your Father.

5. What I'm telling you in darkness you'll repeat again in daylight;
   What you've heard from me in private you must tell it from the housetops!

6. They went forth and preached the gospel, and the sinners were converted,
   They poured oil and healed the people, and they drove out many demons.

Polish hymn
Copyright © 1976 by Willard F. Jabusch

THREE

The Rest of Judea

Bethlehem

Manger Square at the center of Bethlehem is crowded with cars, buses and tourists. Local guides are especially industrious in leading the never-ending stream of visitors into the numerous shops. Pilgrims will find great supplies of olive-wood carvings and some rather bizarre items made from mother-of-pearl.

But who can be surprised at the commercialism in Bethlehem? Don't we think that the Byzantine and Crusader visitors wanted mementos of this town to carry home to their friends and relatives? This is, after all, the town where every day seems to be Christmas. Pilgrims enter the Basilica of the Nativity here and sing "Silent Night" even in the middle of July!

We enter this great fortress of a church through a very low entrance with a fascinating background. Centuries ago, the low doorway

Manger Square and Basilica of the Nativity

The Rest of Judea / 117

was built to keep out the Mamelukes on horse-back. Once through the door, we see the monumental beauty of one of the most ancient churches in the world.

The basilica was built in the sixth century by the Emperor Justinian at the request of the ninety-year-old Saint Sabas who journeyed to Constantinople in 530 with his petition. It rests on an even earlier church built by Constantine in 325. Parts of the Constantinian mosaic pavement can still be seen under some trap doors in the nave. That a well-preserved sixth-century church still stands in the ever-embattled Holy Land must be considered as something of a miracle.

The main altar is hidden by a Greek Orthodox icon stand. However, it is the grotto beneath this altar that really interests us. At the side of the sanctuary steps lead down to a humble place honored as the birthplace of Jesus since A.D. 200. Under a Greek Orthodox altar is a star with the inscription in Latin: "Here Jesus Christ was born of the Virgin Mary." Nearby and a bit lower is the Roman Catholic Altar of the Manger where the Mass of Christmas is offered each morning.

How many pilgrims have come to pray in this stable-cave and to wonder at God's love for humankind! St. Jerome especially loved this place and made Bethlehem his home in the fourth century. Here, he translated the Bible into Latin in a cave reached through the Franciscan Church of St. Catherine. Today, Bethlehem's pilgrims view these places thinking of that ancient census of Emperor Augustus that brought Mary and Joseph to this city of David (Luke 2: 1-10).

Let Us Pray Together

Lord Jesus, you were born here in poverty and cold — a tiny baby, weak and dependent. In these few moments that we spend here, may we be deeply moved by your love and your example.

O Emmanuel, "God who is with us," the babies of the poor and oppressed remind us of you. Those who struggle to provide for their families make us think of Mary and Joseph. May we leave this stable-cave with greater sensitivity and compassion for the least of your brothers and sisters. Amen.

Enter the Stable

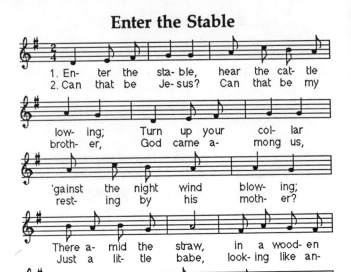

1. En- ter the sta- ble, hear the cat- tle low- ing; Turn up your col- lar 'gainst the night wind blow- ing; There a- mid the straw, in a wood- en man- ger, Ma- ry guards her babe, keep- ing Him from dan- ger.

2. Can that be Je- sus? Can that be my broth- er, God came a- mong us, rest- ing by his moth- er? Just a lit- tle babe, look- ing like an- oth- er, But this lit- tle babe is both God and broth- er!

3. Ah, Virgin Mother, as you rock and feed Him,
   Know that my spirit starves because it needs Him.
I have wandered far, hurt by my delusions,
   Wasting precious time, clutching my confusions.

4. She calls me closer, "Would you like to hold Him?
   Lift Him up gently, in your cloak enfold Him."
Sleeping in my arms, infant so appealing,
   What am I to say, what is now my feeling?

5. Who can resist Him, even hearts long hardened?
   When we surrender, all the past is pardoned.
Never more alone, sterile lives will flourish;
   Jesus is our Bread; only He can nourish!

Traditional carol
Copyright © 1977 by Willard F. Jabusch

Hebron

Hebron, a historic Old Testament town a half-hour south of Bethlehem, is often overlooked by the Christian pilgrim. And that is unfortunate.

It is true that there is no record of Jesus going there. But even though it is off the usual path for pilgrim buses, it would be a shame to miss it.

It is here in this Arab city that we find the magnificently impressive tomb of the Patriarchs and their wives, the ancestors of both Jews and Arabs. Here it was that Abraham bought the cave of Machpelah (Genesis 23: 17-20) as a burial place for his aged wife Sarah. Here too, Abraham himself was buried, followed by his son Isaac with Isaac's wife Rebecca, and by Abraham's grandson Jacob and his wife Leah.

The monumental building, almost a kind of fort, which rises over the burial cave was built by Herod the Great (37-4 B.C.) from enormous blocks of stone. On top of this Justinian built a church in the sixth century and the Crusaders added Gothic vaulting in 1215. From 1267, when this imposing "Haram el-Khalil" ("Shrine of the Friend") was captured by the Sultan Baibars and made into a mosque, only Moslems were allowed to enter.

Only after 1967 were the Jews allocated a place of prayer here. It must surely be the only place where Jews and Moslems pray almost side by side over the bones of their common ancestors.

The huge cenotaphs or tombs of Haram el-Khalil covered in brocade, are also protected with mausoleums. Through their doors and windows, the pious speak their prayers. But it is through an opening in the floor near the wall that the most pious Jews send down their vocal and written petitions directly into the deep cave of Machpelah. It is a bit unnerving for the staid Western visitor to see a woman bending over this opening to the cave and wailing aloud of her

Tomb of Patriarchs, Hebron

grief and her desires far down into the tomb of her ancestors.

It was from Hebron that Joseph set forth to find his brothers (Genesis 37: 14). Here the thirty-year-old David was anointed King of Judah and here he lived until the capture of Jerusalem. His general killed Abner, Saul's general, at Hebron (2 Samuel 3: 27) and David had the two men executed here who had murdered the last son of Saul (2 Samuel 4: 7-11).

Let Us Pray Together

God, one and invisible, great and good, Abraham left his country and his people at your call and came to Hebron. He left the gods and the superstition behind and set forth in faith. He became the ancestor of a mighty people. May all Jews, Moslems and Christians who adore you, the one and true God, learn to live side by side in peace. May Abraham, our common father in faith, be an example of the courage to risk and to believe. Amen.

Leave Your Country and Your People

Refrain

Leave your coun- try and your peo- ple;

Leave your fam- 'ly and your friends;

Trav- el to the land I'll show you;

God will bless the ones he sends.

Verses

1. Go like A- bra- ham be-
2. Some- times God's word is de-

fore you; When he heard the Fa- ther's
mand- ing; Leave se- cur- i- ty you

call, Walk- ing forth in faith and
know; Break- ing ties and bonds that

trust- ing; God is mas- ter of us all.
hold you, When the voice of God says "Go!"

3. Take the path into the desert; Barren seems the rock and sand;
   God will lead you through the desert, When you follow his command:

4. Go with courage up the mountain; Climb the narrow rocky ledge;
   Leave behind all things that hinder; Go with only God as pledge.

Ain Karem
(or Ein Kerem)

Though this picturesque village has become a suburb of Jerusalem, it maintains its charm in a valley of gardens. Tradition says that it was to this village that Mary came to visit her cousin Elizabeth before the birth of John the Baptist.

Certainly the Church of the Visitation, the shrine dedicated to the memory of her visit, is one of the most memorable in the Holy Land. It is surely not big or pretentious, but it is situated on the side of a hill overlooking the village. The view is splendid. Perhaps the fact that one must climb a steep path up the hill adds to the somewhat remote and peaceful atmosphere, the sense

Church of Visitation at Ain Karem

of quiet mystery there. The rather new church is set in a small but lovely garden.

On the lower level of the church are some very old remnants — a well and grotto within a small chapel. The upper church is high and luminous. Its paintings and mosaics have a tranquil joyfulness befitting the happy meeting of the two cousins and the memory of Mary's "Magnificat" (Luke 1: 39).

In fact, Mary's famous prayer is done in tiles on the garden wall in some forty languages.

Down in the town of Ain Karem is the seventeenth-century church honoring the birth of St. John the Baptist. The church of St. John the Baptist contains a crypt which is supposed to be the exact spot where Elizabeth gave birth to John.

One day when I was there, an audacious mouse came out of a crack in the wall and wandered across the star in the floor marking the holy place! So much for getting too serious about exact locations! If a pilgrim's time is limited, it is good to go up the hill to the lovely garden and to the Church of the Visitation, skipping the dreary crypt of John the Baptist and its resident mouse.

Let Us Pray Together
(at the Visitation Chapel)

Lord, your Mother Mary's journey to see Elizabeth was an example of kindness and family solidarity. It was an act that required no little stamina and courage. Even if Mary rode on a donkey, it is a long way from Nazareth to this village in Judea. Help us to value our relatives and friends, and to be loyal to our family. Dispose us to be like your mother — always ready to come and help, to spend time and energy in caring and humble service. Amen.

Angel Gabriel From Heaven

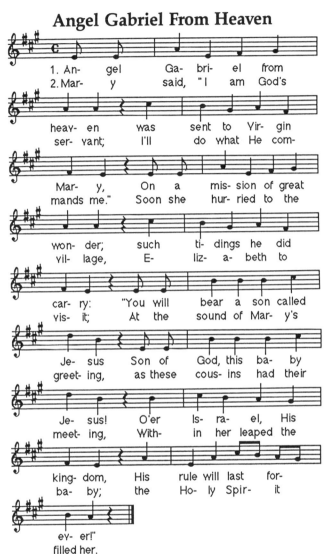

1. An- gel Ga- bri- el from heav- en was sent to Vir- gin Mar- y, On a mis- sion of great won- der; such ti- dings he did car- ry: "You will bear a son called Je- sus Son of God, this ba- by Je- sus! O'er Is- ra- el, His king- dom, His rule will last for- ev- er!"

2. Mar- y said, "I am God's ser- vant; I'll do what He com- mands me." Soon she hur- ried to the vil- lage, E- liz- a- beth to vis- it; At the sound of Mar- y's greet- ing, as these cous- ins had their meet- ing, With- in her leaped the ba- by; the Ho- ly Spir- it filled her.

3. "What an honor my Lord's mother should come to make this visit!
You are favored of all women, and blessed is your baby."
Mary said, "The Lord I'm praising, I rejoice in God, my Savior.
Henceforth all generations will call me blest and happy!"

4. "How he scatters all the haughty and brings down mighty princes;
He has lifted up the lowly and satisfied the hungry;
How he helped his humble servants, in remembrance of his mercy.
His pity he has promised to Abraham forever!"

Let Us Pray Together
(at the Church of John the Baptist)

Jesus, your cousin John said of you: "He must increase; I must decrease." He prepared the way for you, but he had no personal ambition, no need for adulation, no sense of rivalry. May all of us, clergy and laity, be free of competitiveness and bickering in our ministry. Help us all to serve God as best we can in peace and unity. Amen.

Heaven's Kingdom Is Upon You

3. If a tree produces nothing, Cut it down and burn the wood.
   Clear a path, the Lord is coming! Cry aloud as prophets should!

Polish hymn
Copyright © 1978 by Willard F. Jabusch

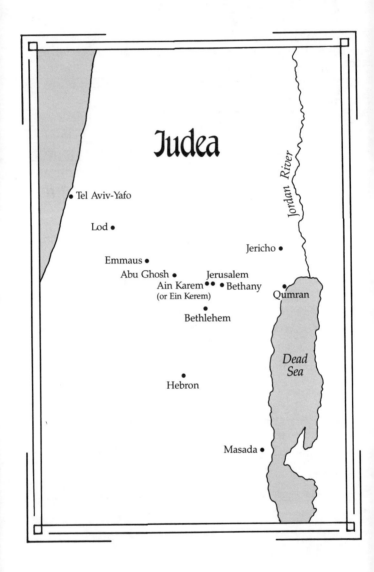

Judea

• Tel Aviv-Yafo

Lod •

Jericho •

Emmaus •

Abu Ghosh •   Jerusalem
Ain Karem •• • Bethany
(or Ein Kerem)   Qumran •
•
Bethlehem

Jordan River

Dead
Sea

•
Hebron

Masada •

Abu Ghosh

No one knows the location of Emmaus, the village where the two disciples recognized the risen Jesus "in the breaking of bread" (Luke 24:13-35). Some feel that the evidence links Emmaus to the village of El Qubeibeh. Others decide in favor of the abandoned Arab village of Amwas near the Trappist monastery of Latrun. There, close to the vineyards that produce grapes for Israel's best wines, are evocative Byzantine ruins that attest to the popularity of the place in the sixth century.

As they approached Jerusalem, however, the Crusaders discovered the spring in the village of Abu Ghosh. They concluded that this must be the site of Emmaus. Here they built a sturdy church, one of the finest surviving examples of Crusader architecture and one of the very few ecclesiastical buildings not destroyed later by the Moslems. Nor was it made into a mosque. Since it was in such an unimportant village and was built directly over the spring, no one seems to have wanted to destroy it.

It still stands with its massive twelfth-century dignity. This church is used each day for the liturgy of the French Benedictines whose monastery garden surrounds the church.

On a hill above the village of Abu Ghosh can be seen a very large and crudely carved statue of Mary. It rises above a French convent and a church erected in 1924 on the remains of a fifth-century Byzantine church. It is "Notre Dame de l'Arche de l'Alliance," "Our Lady of the Ark of the Covenant." We are reminded that the Ark of the Covenant was kept here from time to time in the ancient village of Qiryat Yearim, the predecessor of Abu Ghosh.

Let Us Pray Together

Lord, we know it is not important to discover the precise location of Emmaus. What is important is to hear your words so that, like the two disciples, we can say, "Did not our hearts burn within us as he talked to us on the road . . . ?" May we also be brought out of gloom and discouragement by your presence. And may we also recognize you in the breaking of the bread, good Jesus now risen from the dead. Amen.

One Cloudy Day

1. One cloud-y day we walked a-long, the road was dark and drear-y, Our Mas-ter had been cru-ci-fied, and now our hearts were wear-y, Then came a man who joined us there, he sensed our lone-li-ness and care, He sensed our lone-li-ness and care.

2. Our eyes were kept from see-ing him who by our side was walk-ing; Our fac-es were so full of gloom, and gloom-y was our talk-ing. He asked the cause of our des-pair, the sad-ness that we had to bear, The sad-ness that we had to bear.

3. "Are you alone in all the land the news not fully knowing?
How Jesus Christ took up the cross, to bitter death was going?
He was a prophet great in speech, we longed to hear what He would teach,
   We longed to hear what He would teach.

4. "How dull you are," he answered us, "how slow to hear the prophets.
Was not the Lord to suffer this, before He entered glory?"
Then he explained the Word of God, until we reached a country inn,
   Until we reached a country inn.

5. "Lord, stay with us, the evening comes; we need you here to cheer us;
Come, join us for a bite to eat; how good to have you near us."
He stayed with us and blessed the bread, and then we knew Him as He said.
   And then we knew Him as He said.

Bethany
(El-Azariye)

We always like a town where we have friends, where we can take a warm welcome for granted. Bethany, several miles from Jerusalem, was such a town for Jesus because of his friends, Lazarus, Martha and Mary. He knew he could feel "at home" at their house (Luke 10: 38).

Here in Bethany, Jesus raised Lazarus from the dead (John 11: 11-45) and here, on the last journey from Jericho up to Jerusalem, Jesus stopped for a visit only six days before Passover. On this occasion, Mary anointed Christ's feet although Judas objected to the expense. Jesus defended her extravagant action. On the next day he went over the Mount of Olives and entered Jerusalem riding on a donkey amid the jubilant shouts of the people (Luke 19: 28-38).

The Church of St. Lazarus here was built by the Franciscans in 1953 on much older remains of Byzantine and Crusader buildings. It stands in a pleasant garden back from the road and the shops. It has the form of a large mausoleum although it is not especially dark or depressing. A large inscription in the church is the Latin translation of what Jesus said here in Aramaic: "Ego sum resurrectio et vita." "I am the resurrection and the life."

A bit higher up the road is the reported sepulchre of Lazarus owned by some Moslems. Twenty-four steps lead down to an ancient burial place. Watch your step. It would be easy to fall down the stairs.

Bethany has grown in its many years. A new Greek Orthodox church with a bright blue

Entrance to tomb of Lazarus, Bethany

dome is nearby. There are also a number of new houses and business places. But the Church of St. Lazarus and its garden seem to have retained some of the quiet atmosphere of ancient Bethany.

Let Us Pray Together

Loving God, Jesus performed one of his greatest miracles here when he called forth Lazarus from the grave. Here he said "If anyone believes in me, even though he dies, he will live and whoever lives and believes in me shall never die" (John 11:25). Help us also to believe in Jesus, for we too want to live with him both now and always.

Here at Bethany, Mary poured out her precious perfume. May we generously pour out our time and talents in honor of your Son who lives and reigns with You forever in the unity of the Holy Spirit. Amen.

At Bethany Village

1. At Beth-an-y vil-lage the Lord came to dine, And Mar-tha served sup-per and poured out the wine; But Mar-y brought per-fume, so cost-ly and rare, A-noint-ing his feet which she dried with her hair.

2. The house filled with fra-grance but Ju-das com-plained That she had been waste-ful, her ges-ture dis-dained. Then Je-sus said, "Leave her; she does some-thing fine." Her pour-ing of per-fume, of love was the sign.

Traditional Irish melody
Copyright © 1979 by Willard F. Jabusch

The Jericho Road

Near Jericho east of Jerusalem, it is still possible to walk along parts of an old Roman road which Jesus must have used on his frequent trips between Jerusalem and Jericho. About 14 miles east of Jerusalem, the old Jericho road leads away from the modern highway with its buses and army trucks, and winds down the dry rocky valley called the "Wadi Qilt."

Clinging to the rock wall on the north side of the gorge is the Monastery of St. George begun in the fifth century and still inhabited by a few Greek monks. With the famous Monastery of St. Catherine at the foot of Mount Sinai, this is one of the oldest continuously active places of Christian monastic prayer in the world.

The pilgrim or visitor is allowed to see some ancient icons in the church and to view the cave where monks killed by the Persians in 614 are buried. Centuries seem as nothing in the heat and silence of a place like this. Caves for hermits can be seen above and below the road as it continues down the gorge. A few are once again inhabited by modern followers of the ancient desert ascetics!

But most of all along this original road down to Jericho, one must think of the parable of the Good Samaritan. Did Jesus have a particular inn in mind when he told this wonderful story and fixed this road as its setting? For us, an old caravansary or inn along the modern highway may suggest the necessary stage to conjure up the story even if it dates only from the Turkish period. It is easy to see how robbers could hide among these barren hills and rocks. The black tents and the goats and sheep of nomad shepherds are still found just off the highway. Only a few army posts are a contemporary intrusion.

Jericho

Let Us Pray Together

Jesus, you knew the impact your parable would have because you made the hero a Samaritan. In your time, Samaritans were so despised by the Jews. In our century, you might have told of an Ulster Protestant stopping to help a Catholic after a bishop and a nun had passed by. Or, the story might have told of a Palestinian Moslem stopping to help a Jew after a rabbi and a kibbutz member had ignored him. Lord, you taught us vividly that we are to reach out in kindness even to our enemies. May we have the strength to do so. Amen.

On the Jericho Highway

1. When a trav-el-er
   fell a-mong thieves, on the Jer-i-cho
   high-way,
   Thieves who beat him and took what he
   had, They left him nak-ed and bleed-ing,
   When a trav-el-er
   fell a-mong thieves, on the Jer-i-cho
   high-way.

2. Then a priest and a
   le-vite passed by, on the Jer-i-cho
   high-way,
   Nei-ther stopped on their way to give
   help, They passed him by in a hur-ry,
   Then a priest and a
   le-vite passed by, on the Jer-i-cho
   high-way.

3. Then there came a Samaritan man, who was moved with compassion,
   He got down and he bandaged his wounds, He cared for him like a brother,
   Then there came a Samaritan man, who was moved with compassion.

4. Then he lifted him on his own mount, to an innkeeper brought him,
   "Here is money, and on my way back, I'll pay you more for your trouble."
   Then he lifted him on his own mount, to an innkeeper brought him.

5. Which of these was a neighbor indeed, on the Jericho highway?
   He with pity who bothered to stop, Who saw his brother's condition.
   Which of these was a neighbor indeed, on the Jericho highway?

Jericho

Ancient Jericho is below sea level, surrounded by an arid and sun-blasted landscape. This old city could not exist without the generous waters of its spring, but those life-giving waters have never failed Jericho. For many centuries, they have made this the world's most famous oasis and probably its oldest inhabited city.

The ancient settlement has been sliced into by the archaeologists like a giant layer cake. Successive layers of buildings and cultures have been revealed. Even for the pilgrim who is strictly a non-expert, this is an impressive and educational "dig." The gushing waters close by continue to irrigate the famous Jericho oranges, grapefruit, bananas, figs and dates which are sold along the streets. In summer, the fresh cool orange juice, which comes from Jericho, becomes an absolute necessity!

The pyramids of Egypt are four thousand years younger than the great tower of Jericho. This means that the town was already old when it was captured by Joshua (Joshua 2-6). Even Elijah and Elisha stopped by here (2 Kings 2). Herod turned the place into his winter residence, a kind of Palm Springs or Sun City in ancient Palestine. For Jesus, it was a convenient stopping place when he came down from Galilee along the valley of the Jordan. By following the valley road from the Lake of Galilee, the inhospitable land of Samaria could be avoided completely.

Here too Jesus was hailed as "the son of David," and here he healed the blind man (Luke

Caves At Qumran

18: 35-43). This was also the home of Zacchaeus, the short tax collector, in whose house Jesus dined (Luke 19: 1-10).

Near this city, close to the Dead Sea, the famous caves and settlement of Qumran were found by a Bedouin shepherd boy in 1947. These caves yielded the oldest manuscripts of the Bible. The oasis of En Gedi ("Goats' Spring") with its memories of David and Saul (l Samuel 24: 2-23) is also not far from old Jericho. Pilgrims can also see the great fortress of Masada on its hilltop here. All these lie to the south on the road to Eilat and the Gulf of Aqaba.

Let Us Pray Together

"Jesus, Son of David, have pity on me!" We make the prayer of the Jericho blind man our own, dear Lord. It is simple and to the point. We too need your mercy, your healing and your caring love. "Lord, that I may see." For though we may see physically, our spiritual blindness can be cured only by your power. May we too look up from the dust and recognize your holy face. May the darkness give way to your light. And may we praise and thank you every day of our lives. Amen.

Son of David

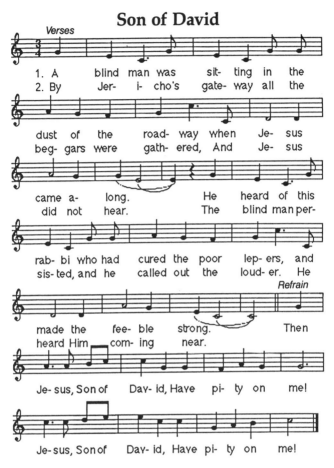

Verses

1. A blind man was sit- ting in the dust of the road- way when Je- sus came a- long. He heard of this rab- bi who had cured the poor lep- ers, and made the fee- ble strong.

2. By Jer- i- cho's gate- way all the beg- gars were gath- ered, And Je- sus did not hear. The blind man per- sis- ted, and he called out the loud- er. He heard Him com- ing near.

Refrain

Then Je- sus, Son of Dav- id, Have pi- ty on me!

Je- sus, Son of Dav- id, Have pi- ty on me!

3. "Your shouting disturbs Him," the disciples said firmly,
   "Would you disturb the peace?"
   He was not discouraged, and his voice became bolder,
   His prayer he would not cease.

4. "The Master is busy and is not to be bothered:
   He has no time for you!"
   But now Jesus heard him, and he said to the blind man:
   "What would you have me do?"

5. The blind man took courage, for he said to the Savior:
   "O, Lord, that I may see!"
   His eyes saw the sunlight and the face of his Master,
   From darkness now set free.

The Mount of Temptation

The traditional site of Jesus' fast of forty days is a stark and forbidding mountain to the west of Jericho. It is called the Mount of Quarantine (Mount of Forty). There are more than enough stones in this region to illustrate Satan's words uttered here. "'If you are the Son of God, tell these stones to turn into loaves.' But he replied, 'Scripture says: Man does not live on bread alone, but on every word that comes from the mouth of God.' " (Matthew 4: 2-4).

A chapel was built on the summit of this mountain in A.D. 340, but it was not until 1895 that the Greek Orthodox built their monastery half way up. There is a difficult pathway from the monastery up to the remains of the fourth-century chapel. Frankly, most pilgrims are content to look at the somber mountain from afar!

Mount of Quarantine

Let Us Pray Together

Most kind God, it is important for us to remember that your Son and our Savior was fully human. Here in the desert, he experienced the insidious pull of temptation. Three times he was presented with evil in the guise of something good. Three times he exposed the deceit and remained loyal to you.

In your wisdom, you allowed your Son to be tried by temptation. May we also turn from what is evil toward what is good. We ask this in the name of Jesus. Amen.

Jesus Sought Out the Desert

1. Je- sus sought out the des- ert,
2. Can we with Je- sus tra- vel

for- ty long days to fast,
in- to a des- ert place?

Climbed up the bar- ren moun- tain,
Fast- ing and ev- er plead- ing,

reach- ing the top at last.
seek- ing the Fa- ther's grace?

Spent all His time in pray- ing,
One with Him in our pray- ing,

ask- ing His Fa- ther's will,
mak- ing His words our own,

Soon to be- gin His mis- sion,
When we ask bread to feed us,

pro- phe- cies to ful- fill.
God will not give a stone.

3. Christ had to face temptation, three times did Satan speak.
When Christ was weak and hungry, Satan His soul did seek.
Jesus withstood his tempting, strong was He, good and wise,
Showing us how to conquer, under the desert skies.

Old Basque melody
Copyright © 1976, 1986 by Willard F. Jabusch

FOUR

Galilee, Samaria and the Seacoast

Nazareth:
Basilica of the
Annunciation

The Basilica of the Annunciation in Nazareth is the largest and most important contemporary church building in Israel. Some would
say, however, that this Marian shrine is an enormous and outrageously expensive artistic failure.
It does seem designed to overwhelm the visitor.
First impressions of it are usually confused and
disquieting. Perhaps pilgrims sense it is all too
much—too much marble, too many madonnas,
too many national styles, too many altars. One
wishes for the chaste beauty of the church of St.
Anne in Jerusalem, the quiet darkness of the
monastery church at Abu Ghosh or the solem-
nity of the great Justinian basilica at Bethlehem.
Nonetheless, this is the shrine dedicated to the
sublime mystery of the Incarnation and to the
moment when a maiden of Nazareth said her
simple "yes" to God in profound humility.

Yet in the lower church, the distractions and
disappointments are fewer. We are down at the
level of the Byzantine and Crusader constructions where the focal point is a simple cave. Tradition places the annunciation scene here, and
one senses the simplicity and beauty of Mary re-
ceiving the message of the angel. She learned
that she was to be the mother of the Messiah.
"Hail, full of grace!"

For so many centuries, Christians have
knelt and prayed here in wonder and thanksgiving. God so loved the world that he sent his only

son to us. And Mary, the pure and holy girl from Nazareth, was ready to say, "Behold the handmaid of the Lord."

Christianity begins here in the meeting of God's love and a girl's obedience.

Cave of Annunciation

Let Us Pray Together

God our Father, we admit it. We will never understand the mystery of your love and willingness to save us. We will never appreciate fully what happened here in this cave in Nazareth. We can never give adequate thanks for the Incarnation.

We can say once again that we want to return your love. We can feel here a fresh astonishment that the baby who grew in the womb of Mary was your Son. And we can think with joyful wonder that you will dwell within us too, making each a living temple of God. May we never forget the dignity Jesus has given us by coming here as our brother and friend. Amen.

Blessed Are You

Bless- ed are you, Mar- y,
You gave God a dwell- ing,

Moth- er of our Sav- ior mak- er of the
in your womb you car- ried Je- sus 'til his

Verses

stars and earth; 1. God sent his own
day of birth. 2. "Greet- ings, O most

an- gel to a love- ly maid- en
fa- vored, tru- ly God is with you,

In the town of Naz- a- reth,
You'll con- ceive and bear a son!

with a won- drous mes- sage for a girl called
You will call him Je- sus, he will rule for-

Mar- y, In the town of Naz- a-
ev- er, Ho- ly King and God's own

reth.
Son."

3. "Here am I," said Mary, "I am God's poor servant;
    As you say, then let it be!
  God looks on his handmaid; though she be so humble,
    Kindly has he dealt with me."

4. Arrogant are scattered, monarchs tumble downward,
    But the poor are lifted high;
  Wealthy hands go empty, but God feeds the hungry;
    Surely he will heed their cry.

Hungarian hymn

Copyright © 1979 by Willard F. Jabusch

Nazareth:
Church of St. Joseph

Some Nazareth tour guides take pains to show pilgrims a cistern, rock stairway and other indications of an early house and cellar. They link these, all in the crypt of the Church of St. Joseph, to the Holy Family. But no one can really say with certainty that Mary, Joseph and Jesus did live here.

If not here, then their little home and Joseph's carpentry shop must have been nearby. Nazareth was a small and unimportant town at that time. Excavations show that the houses were clustered in this area.

Certainly the quiet beauty of St. Joseph's church is as good a place as any to think of the youthful Jesus. Near this site, he grew up surrounded by the love and example of Joseph, the humble workman and foster father and by Mary, his lovely young mother.

We know so little about those years of Jesus' childhood and adolescence. The pious imagination will always and understandably try to fill in the blanks. But from what Jesus said and did as an adult we can have no doubt that he learned much in his earlier years. Clearly, he was raised as a good Jew in a devout and loving family.

Since Joseph is not mentioned at the end of Christ's life, it is presumed that he died before the public life of Christ began. Did he die in the arms of Jesus and Mary? Did Jesus keep the carpentry shop open for a while to support his widowed mother? When did he tell her that he had to leave to start his itinerant ministry of preaching and healing?

Such questions come to one praying and thinking in St. Joseph's Church in Nazareth. The thirty years of Christ's hidden life remain hidden. But here we do feel closer to the young Jesus, to his holy mother and to the faithful and good-hearted carpenter who had such a formative role in the early life of our Savior.

Let Us Pray Together

Lord Jesus, the evangelists either knew little about your early years or did not find it important to describe them. We are left to wonder what your boyhood and youth were like in that sleepy provincial town of Nazareth. Here you learned to pray, to read the Scriptures, to work with Joseph and Mary, to discover the beauty of nature and the mysteries of the human heart. Lord, be with the children and young people of our time. Protect them from harm and help them also to grow in grace and wisdom as you did. Amen.

In Nazareth of Galilee

1. In Na- za- reth of Gal- i- lee, The
2. He was like us in ev- 'ry- thing, He

Son of Mar- y grew to be A
learned the les- sons life must bring; Temp-

man both strong and gen- tle too, All
ta- tion, doubt, he felt them all, yet

knew the kind- ly things he'd do.
in- to sin he did not fall.

3. He was a carpenter by trade; All things of wood he gladly made.
   With care he'd fashion chair or bed, Some humble work to earn
   his bread.

4. The world was then as it is now, So full of those who wonder how
   Someone with joy can give his youth Obeying God in love and truth.

5. When Joseph died, he felt the pain, The winter wind and driving rain;
   He had to leave his mother too, He had his Father's work to do.

6. Then after thirty years or so, It was the time to rise and go,
   For he would do his Father's will, And all our deepest hopes fulfill.

German melody
Copyright © 1985 by Willard F. Jabusch

Synagogue of Nazareth

Nazareth pilgrims will want to walk west of the Basilica of the Annunciation into the old part of town to the Synagogue Church. It is a simple stone building which tradition says is the synagogue in which the holy family of Nazareth attended sabbath services.

This is certainly a very old building. And it is a suitable place to consider the influence which Mary, Joseph and the whole Jewish community had on the young Jesus. Joseph would have taken Jesus with him to the synagogue just as Orthodox Jewish fathers take their sons today.

The whole synagogue experience would have had a very powerful effect on Jesus. The reading of the Torah and the singing of the psalms would impress any sensitive boy, especially when reinforced by the prayers and pious rituals of the home.

Today as then, Judaism is much more than doctrine. It is a way of life which involves the whole family. At first glance, Judaism seems to be very much a "man's religion" with fathers deeply involved in the religious education of sons. But it also depends on the customs and atmosphere of orthodox practice and piety maintained by the mother in the home.

In subtle ways and in very public ways, the whole Jewish community of Nazareth molded the religious sensibilities of the town's young people. It seems likely that "the carpenter's son" was no exception.

Let Us Pray Together

Jesus, your human attitudes were deeply formed by Mary, Joseph and by the religious practice of Nazareth. Help parents to realize the importance of their words and example. Help us all to know that our faith and devotion, or lack of it, strongly influence the next generation. For we are all responsible for one another. Even the most independent young people secretly look for guidance and example from parents, older relatives and from friends. Keep us from giving scandal. Make us humble and honest models of Christian living. Amen.

When Mary Lit the Candles

1. When Mar- y lit the can- dles as
2. Each sab- bath all were go- ing to

dark- ness cov- ered the land, Her
syn- a- gogue in the town, So

son could hear her pray- ing and
Je- sus went with Jo- seph and

watch her gen- tle hand; In
with the men sat down; He

Naz- a- reth he learned by heart the
lis- tened to the word of God and

prayer that his moth- er would sing; 1-4: From
joined in the sing- ing of psalms;

Jo- seph and Mar- y he learned the ways of

prayer.

3. Each day began when Joseph would offer blessings aloud;
   He followed Jewish custom and praised the name of God;
   And Jesus learned the words to say to thank Him for all that He gives;

4. From Galilee they traveled to celebrate the great feast;
   They saw the temple gilded with sunshine from the east.
   They sang the hymns that pilgrims sing who climb to the temple of God;

Polish hymn
Copyright © 1979 by Willard F. Jabusch

Mount Tabor

Not far from Nazareth, Mount Tabor rises alone and majestic above the farms and villages of Galilee. The outline of the great church, the Basilica of the Transfiguration, can be seen from the highway far below. It is a place of grandeur and remote mysticism, a worthy setting for the wondrous experience of the transfiguration of Christ and the approving voice of God.

But was it this mountain? Certainly this was a "High Place" for the Canaanites who worshipped Baal in the second millennium before Christ. At the time of the Judges in the twelfth century before Christ, the prophetess Deborah gathered troops here to defeat the general Sisera with his fearful chariots and soldiers (Judges 4: 12-16).

From the fourth century after Christ, the description of the transfiguration was connected with this isolated mountaintop, Mount Tabor (Matthew 17; Mark 9: 2-13; Luke 9: 28-36). Over

Mount Tabor from a distance

the centuries, many chapels and monasteries have been built and destroyed here. The present Franciscan church designed by Antonio Barluzzi in the style of Syrian churches of the fifth century is a truly noble building. The apsidal vault contains a splendid mosaic of the transfiguration showing Christ with Moses and Elijah. Far below the church and monastery can be seen the verdant plain of Jezreel and the mountains of Samaria.

But this is not an easily reached mountaintop! The road is narrow, sinuous and poorly marked. Let drivers beware!

Let Us Pray Together

Jesus, we say with an overwhelmed Peter, "Lord, it is good for us to be here." It is good in this land where you lived as a man to be reminded that you are also the Son of God. Many events and places in the Holy Land make it clear that you were truly human. On this mountain we are also made aware of your divinity. You are the beloved Son of the heavenly Father. For a moment, Peter, James and John saw your divine splendor shine forth and knew you to be Lord of the law and the prophets.

We praise you as the Second Person of the Blessed Trinity, as our all-holy Savior. We fall to our knees, O Jesus Christ, and adore you as God. We trust in your divine power and rely upon your undefeated love. Be with us forever. Amen.

Come to the Mountain

1-4: Come to the moun-tain of the Lord, to the moun- tain.

1. Christ ap- pears in
   splen- did ar- ray,
   And His glo- ry
   bright- ens our day.

2. For His gar- ments
   glis- ten like snow,
   And His face is
   bright as the sun.

3. Moses and Elias are near;
   Lord, it's good for us to be here!

4. On Mount Tabor Christ lets us see
   What a glimpse of Heaven must be.

Israeli folksong
Copyright © 1966, 1981 by Willard F. Jabusch

Cana
(Kafr Kanna)

Cana in Galilee is a homespun town not far from Nazareth. At a village wedding feast here, Jesus worked his first miracle at the request of his mother. Perhaps more commercialism and bigger shrines could therefore be expected here. It is true that a few shops offer bottles of "wine from Cana" as pleasant souvenirs. One shopkeeper says his wine comes in two flavors, "sweet and sweet-sweet." But Cana people are friendly country people, and both Christians and Moslems welcome the small number of pilgrims who find their way here.

On Sundays, the "children's Mass" in the Franciscan church, the Cana wedding site, is full of lively boys and girls. An elderly friar shuffles

Cana's "water jug" at Franciscan Church

Galilee, Samaria and the Seacoast / 161

down the aisle to the altar. Old ladies in black finger their rosaries but exchange bits of village gossip at the same time. Pilgrims feel at home in Cana.

This is a place for all of us to pray for all married people so that the hope and trust that brought them to their wedding day may not decay. Especially this is the place for husband and wife to pause and ask for a still deeper love and faithfulness until the end.

Let Us Pray Together

O Lord Jesus, the first of the wonders which you performed in your public life was done to save a young couple from embarrassment. May we also experience your care and kindness. Here you changed ordinary water into choice wine. Please change the mediocrity of our lives into something beautiful and precious. May we all be blessed through the intercession of your kind mother, as others were here at Cana in Galilee so long ago. Amen.

Jesus Gives to Us His Word

Verses

1. Fill the emp- ty wa- ter jars 'til they're ov- er
2. From your dark- ened tomb come forth, once a- gain you're

flow- ing. Wa- ter made the best of wines to the guests is go- ing.
walk- ing! Turn from all that's cold and dead, with the Lord start talk- ing.

Refrain

Je- sus gives to us his word, When we pray we're sure- ly heard. And he gives us faith, And he gives us hope, And his love, and his love, And his love we're shar- ing, Nev- er more des- pair- ing.

Catalonian melody
Copyright © 1979 by Willard F. Jabusch

Galilee, Samaria and the Seacoast / 163

Mount of the Beatitudes

Pilgrims to this spot will wonder if there is a more beautiful place. Is there a finer view than the Mount of the Beatitudes? From the arcaded porch around the church there, you will see the Sea of Galilee far below. There too is the road to Capernaum and the orchards and farms. This mount is a place of silence and sunshine, of such loveliness and cool breezes. It is not hard to think of this hill as the place where some of the most beautiful Gospel words were spoken.

Pilgrims should sit on the steps of the garden in the sun or find a bench under the old trees and read Matthew 5-7. Nowhere in the Holy Land does the heart find itself more easily lifted up. Nowhere can there be found a better place for inner healing and renewed hope.

The Church of the Beatitudes was built only in 1937. It is an octagonal building with a dome reminiscent of St. Peter's in Rome. But there is an admirable simplicity in the design. The Italian architect Barluzzi allowed classic forms to be modestly expressed in local basalt and the white stone of Nazareth. Latin inscriptions in the church spell out the eight Beatitudes on the eight faces of the church interior (Matthew 5: 3-10).

Behind the church stands an older pilgrims' hospice cared for by Italian nuns. Although the spartan rooms can be freezing in the winter, a summer stay can be delightful. The pasta is good any time of the year, and the sisters' hospitality is warm and genuine.

Chapel of Beatitudes, Galilee

Let Us Pray Together

Good Jesus, the crowds sat down in the grass on this hillside to hear you. Even the magnificent view could not distract them, for you were there to teach and to cheer them. They treasured your words and kept them in their hearts.

Lord, we would hear you speak to us today. May your words enter deeply into our hearts and into our lives.

Again in our time, so many are persecuted for your sake. Once again there is need for peacemakers, for the pure of heart, for those who hunger and thirst for justice. May we be found among them and share with them in your kingdom. Amen.

The Folk the World Considers Least

1. The folk the world con- sid- ers
2. If you're a sin- ner, don't des-

least, The Lord has called to his
pair; Our Host will show you a

joy- ful feast. Good things are wait- ing,
spec- ial care. He makes you feel a

well pre- pared; His food and
wel- come guest; Your heart re-

drink with us are shared.
newed and ful- ly blest!

3. Are you alone, without a friend,
   Confused, not knowing how life will end?
   For you He keeps an honored place;
   He sees your heart and knows your face.

4. Have you a heart that's full of pain,
   Unable happiness to regain?
   This banquet helps to make you strong;
   New joy and peace will come along!

5. The poor and humble will be fed;
   The Lord with sinners would break the bread;
   Take up the cup He gives for drink;
   God's ways are not what people think!

Tabgha

In 1932, two Germans, Mader and Schneider, came upon a splendid mosaic floor not far from Capernaum on the Sea of Galilee. The mosaic was hidden under centuries of dirt and rubble. When it was uncovered it was clear that it was all that remained of a fifth-century basilica honoring the miracle of the loaves and fishes (Mark 6: 30-44). A new church in the basilica style was built over the mosaic floor by German Benedictines and consecrated in 1982. The wonderful floor with its delightful ducks, herons, snakes and flamingoes and its early representation of the loaves and fishes near the altar is being carefully restored by young German workers.

It is no surprise that several Christian sites are clustered in this area. Our forefathers and mothers had no automobiles or buses and did not like to walk any further than was necessary. So why not establish the shrine in honor of this miracle of the loaves and fishes near others dedicated to the sermon on the mount and the primacy of Peter? The new church here, simple and strong, not only protects an ancient mosaic floor of great historical and artistic importance, but also provides one of the Holy Land's most beautiful spaces for Christian prayer and song.

And, a few steps away up near the road, there is a modest restaurant perfectly suitable for lunch. Somehow it seems right to order some bread and fish! Even if you do not ordinarily say grace before or after meals, here where Jesus fed the crowds out of kindness may be a good place to start.

Let Us Pray Together

Lord, from earliest times our Christian ancestors
have prayed here in gratitude for the multiplication of
the loaves and fishes, a symbol of the Holy Eucharist.
You do not leave us hungry, Lord. Rather than bread
and fish, you now give us yourself as our holy food
and drink. We stand in awe before the mystery of your
tender love. Nourish us with your gifts lest we die in
the wilderness. Amen.

Five Thousand People

Brightly

1. Five thou- sand peo- ple sat down on the
2. Here stands a boy with a bas- ket of

grass- y ground, Five thou- sand peo- ple sat
bar- ley loaves, Here stands a boy with a

down all a- round. Mas- ter how
few lit- tle fish. How can we

can we feed them far from a
feed the peo- ple, how can we

town or vil- lage; Mas- ter, how
sat- is- fy them, How can we

can we give them some- thing to eat?
feed them all with two lit- tle fish?

Five thou- sand peo- ple sat down on the
Here stands a boy who has brought fish and

ground.
bread.

3. Saying a blessing the Lord gave those barley loaves,
   Saying a blessing the Lord gave the fish.
   Ev'ryone ate their fill there, up on that grassy hill there,
   Ev'ryone had enough to share in the feast.
   Saying a blessing the Lord broke the bread.

Galilee, Samaria and the Seacoast / 169

Chapel of the Primacy of Peter

Built over fourth-century foundations at the very edge of the Sea of Galilee near Capernaum stands the Chapel of the Primacy of Peter. This black basalt chapel put up by the Franciscans in 1933 now has new stained–glass windows and a simple white interior. A Spanish lady who came here about A.D. 400 described the steps cut into the rock by the lake here as "those on which the Lord stood." At any rate, it is here that we commemorate the appearance of the risen Christ to the apostles. Here we think not only of the forgiveness offered to the cowardly Peter but of the special responsibility which Jesus gave him. "Feed my lambs. Feed my sheep" (John 21: 15-17).

Chapel of the Primacy of Peter on Sea of Galilee

There are many places along the lake, the Sea of Galilee, where the pilgrim can view the water and even get close to it, but none better than this spot. How good it is to sit here near the little chapel and look out over the lake that figures so prominently in the Gospels, but in such a powerful way in the last chapter of John.

Was it here that the resurrected Jesus cooked breakfast for his apostles after their long night of fishing (John 21: 9-11)? Was it here that Peter dived into the water and swam to shore in order to be the first on the beach? Was the smell of the frying fish carried on the wind out to the boat to make the apostles hungry? What did the voice of Jesus sound like here in the open air as he spoke to them the words they would never forget?

Let Us Pray Together

Jesus, we feel near to you here in this simple beautiful place. For a time we can let our worries and fears be blown away by the breeze off the Sea of Galilee. We can think with love and longing of you, our dear Brother and Friend. You forgave Peter here and gave him important work to do. Forgive us the cowardly moments of our lives. Call us to do something good and beautiful for you. Let us leave this lovely place resolved to be more generous in your service and more open to the good inspirations which you send us. Amen.

Do You Love Me?

Verses

1. Pe- ter de- nied that he knew Je- sus,
2. Pe- ter re- ceived com- plete for- give- ness

swore that he nev- er saw the man;
for all his fol- ly and his sin;

But on the lake- shore that spring
Shep- herds must al- so be for-

morn- ing, this is the way that Christ be-
giv- en-- then their great mis- sion can be-

Refrain

gan: "Si- mon, son of John,
gin!

do you love me more than these?" "Oh,

Lord, you know that I love

you." "Then feed my lambs."
sheep."

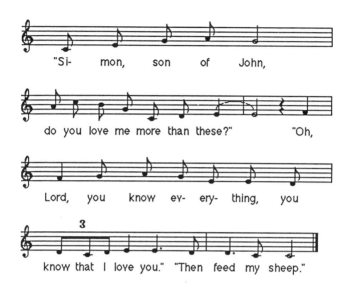

"Si- mon, son of John,

do you love me more than these?" "Oh,

Lord, you know ev- ery- thing, you

know that I love you." "Then feed my sheep."

3. Are we, like Peter, so discouraged,
   full of remorse and full of shame?
   Jesus will ask us this same question;
   Jesus will treat us just the same.

Cf. John 21: 15-19
Copyright © 1976, 1986 by Willard F. Jabusch

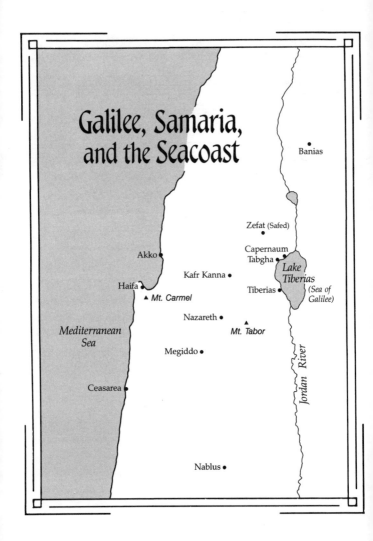

Galilee, Samaria, and the Seacoast

Banias

Zefat (Safed)

Akko

Capernaum
Tabgha

Lake Tiberias
(Sea of Galilee)

Kafr Kanna

Haifa

Tiberias

▲ *Mt. Carmel*

Nazareth

▲
Mt. Tabor

Mediterranean Sea

Megiddo

Jordan River

Ceasarea

Nablus

Capernaum

If Jesus can be said to have had a home after he left Nazareth at the beginning of his "public life," it would have to be Capernaum, a fishing town at the northern edge of the lake. St. Matthew says that he came and dwelt here (Matthew 4: 13).

Here the sturdy fishermen, Peter, Andrew, James and John heard the call to follow him (Matthew 4: 18-22). The miracles Jesus worked here seem to have been numerous. We remember especially the curing of the Roman centurion's servant (Luke 7: 5-10) and that poignant scene when he raised the daughter of Jairus, a ruler of the local synagogue, from the dead (Luke 8: 40-56).

Motor launches from Tiberias now put in at the Capernaum pier. How many times did Jesus and his fishermen come ashore from their boats here and receive the hospitality of Peter's family?

In ancient times, an octagonal shrine was built over the place and many early pious inscriptions were found here. As a result, we have a good idea that this is where Peter lived and where Jesus healed Peter's mother-in-law. In fact, 131 first-century inscriptions were found here. On these reconstructed plaster fragments, the names of Jesus and Peter were frequently mentioned. They indicate that this house was already revered as the "House of Peter the Apostle" (Luke 4: 38-41); (Matthew 8: 14-17); (Mark 1: 29-31).

The beautiful Capernaum synagogue that we see just beyond the "Octagon of St. Peter" was built only at the end of the fourth century. But in all probability, it was constructed over the earlier synagogue where Jesus "taught them with authority" (Mark 1: 21-22).

The ruins of Capernaum have been in the control of the Franciscans for over ninety years. The Franciscans have promoted scholarly study of the remains and have themselves conducted important excavations. But much of the original town still lies buried beneath the dirt and grasses.

Holy Land pilgrims who come fifty years from now will better understand the town where Jesus lived and performed wonders during his last three years. Even now, beautiful stone fragments of carvings, old olive presses, the great trees and the flowers cascading over the walls help make this a place for tranquil reflection. When a breeze comes off the lake, it is not difficult to picture the ancient fishermen's boats. Along the shoreline, one can almost hear them ask Jesus: "Where do you live?" "Come and see," he answered (John 1: 39).

"House of Peter," Capernaum

Let Us Pray Together

Lord Jesus, you found your apostles in the humble fishermen of this town. They had little education, no sophistication, few pretensions. But you chose them. You called them from their boats and nets, giving them the strength they would need to live and die for you.

We have also heard you call us, Lord. Like the fishermen of Capernaum, we are also attached to our "boats and nets," our familiar lifestyles. We do not leave them easily. We need courage, Master. We need faith to believe that you can use the likes of us in your holy work. Amen.

All Night They Had Been Fishing

1. All night they had been fish- ing, out
2. They heard him give an or- der, "Push

on the si- lent lake; The morn- ing chill cut
out in- to the deep; Cast out up- on the

through them, no fish was there to
right side once more be- fore you

take, When sud- den- ly up-
sleep!" They cast their nets, his

on the shore toward which they pulled their
word o- beyed, and such a catch they

heav- y oar, They saw a man who
quick- ly made, Their nets were far too

called them, "Now chil- dren have you
heav- y. Then John cried out, "It

caught some fish?" "Oh, no," they an- swered
is the Lord." The morn- ing now was

sad- ly.
break- ing.

Dutch melody
Copyright © 1977 by Willard F. Jabusch

The Jordan River

Unfortunately, it is no longer easy for pilgrims to visit the places along the Jordan River which commemorate the baptism of Christ and the ministry of John the Baptist (John 3). Permission can be obtained from the police, but the average pilgrim is not inclined to bother. The whole area has been declared a military zone because the 200-mile-long river forms part of the frontier with the Kingdom of Jordan. Therefore, Christian pilgrims must satisfy themselves with a visit to the Jordan river in the north where it flows out of the Lake of Galilee. Many go there to pour a bit of Jordan water over their heads in memory of their own baptism. Some are actually baptized along the bank, usually by immersion.

Although the baptism of Jesus certainly

Jordan River

Galilee, Samaria and the Seacoast / 179

took place further south, closer to Jericho and the Dead Sea, even the northern portions of the river are fascinating. The Jordan's water makes possible the orchards and verdant farms in the valley. It is the flowing stream that allows the trees and grasses to grow where a desert would otherwise exist. The Jordan is the ageless symbol of God's abundant love and grace. Even a handful of its cool water refreshes our forehead in the summer heat.

Let Us Pray Together

O God, it is many years since most of us were "born again of water and the Holy Spirit." If we were only babies at baptism, the baptismal promises were made in our names. But now, here by the Jordan River, we want to ratify those promises and renew our covenant with you. We renounce Satan and all his deceit. We renounce the ways of selfishness and shame, of fear and slavery.

We give ourselves to you and love you with all our mind and heart and will. We trust in the cross and resurrection of your Son Jesus Christ who brings us freedom from our chains. We know that he lifts our yoke of sadness and is our Way, our Truth and our Life.

We dedicate the years that remain and our talents and our energy to building up your kingdom of peace and holiness. We will tell those who are poor in body and spirit that you want them to be free and happy forever.

We hope in your promises and rejoice in your kindness. You have washed away our guilt in the waters of Baptism and we thank you in the name of Jesus. Amen.

Bright in the Sunshine

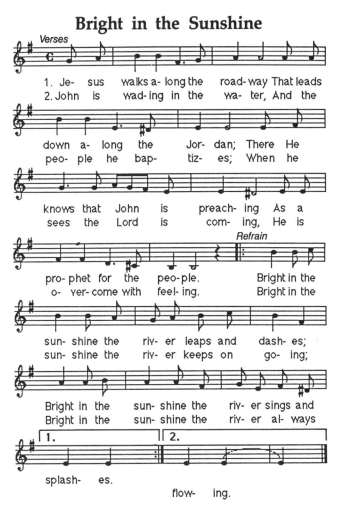

Verses

1. Je- sus walks a- long the road- way That leads
2. John is wad- ing in the wa- ter, And the

down a- long the Jor- dan; There He
peo- ple he bap- tiz- es; When he

knows that John is preach- ing As a
sees the Lord is com- ing, He is

Refrain

pro- phet for the peo- ple. Bright in the
o- ver- come with feel- ing. Bright in the

sun- shine the riv- er leaps and dash- es;
sun- shine the riv- er keeps on go- ing;

Bright in the sun- shine the riv- er sings and
Bright in the sun- shine the riv- er al- ways

1. splash- es.

2. flow- ing.

3. Jesus wades out in the Jordan, So that John may there baptize Him;
As His cousin pours the water, Jesus humbly stands before him.

4. If you enter in these waters, You will rise to life forever;
You will share the life of Jesus, And will dwell within His Kingdom.

Castillian melody
Copyright © 1979 by Willard F. Jabusch

Banias
(Caesarea Philippi)

Busloads of Israeli schoolchildren are often seen heading to field trips at a place once called Caesarea Philippi. The ancient site, now called Banias, has other appeals as well. Families often find this a pleasant spot to picnic along the river here in northern Israel. A place of abundant springs once considered sacred to the god Pan (Paneas), Banias is once again populated and alive. On gray winter days, Banias or Caesarea Philippi can be cold and remote. The snowy peak of Mount Hermon, the nearby Lebanese border and the rough-looking Golan Heights up the winding road to the east give Banias a strategic importance.

The statues of the lascivious Pan are gone but the niches which held them are still clearly seen carved out of the cliffs above the gushing springs here. Even before the cult of Pan in Hellenistic times, this dramatic site was a center for the worship of Baal. By the time of Jesus, Philip, a son of King Herod, had built his capital here and named it Caesarea to flatter the emperor. To avoid confusion with the port of Caesarea on the Mediterranean, this town was called Caesarea Philippi from then on. Its ruins are still covered with the dirt of centuries. Together with nearby Tel Dan, the capital of the Tribe of Dan and source of the Jordan River, Caesarea Philippi awaits the shovels of archaeologists.

A sadly abandoned Catholic church on the road toward the Golan Heights is the sole reminder that Jesus came here (Matthew 16: 13-20) and promised Peter the keys of the kingdom of heaven.

From this passage, of course, comes the text which is inscribed in huge Latin and Greek letters around the inside of St. Peter's in Rome. "You are Peter and on this rock I will build my Church." But unhappily, the varied interpretations of these words of Jesus have led Christians into serious divisions and bitter arguments for many years.

In this scenic and historic place it would be good, therefore, to pray for unity and forgiveness, asking that "all might be one." May Catholics, Orthodox and Protestants allow ancient antagonisms and suspicions to be washed away in the constantly clear and flowing waters from the springs of Banias.

Let Us Pray Together

Jesus, when you declared that Peter was the rock on which you would build your church, you did not want your words to be an excuse for rivalry and separation. Bring together in love all who call upon you as their Savior. Help us to forget the battles of the past and to work with one mind and heart to make this world a place where it is easier to be good. May we help each other to follow the path of holiness and humble service. Amen.

I Saw a Stream

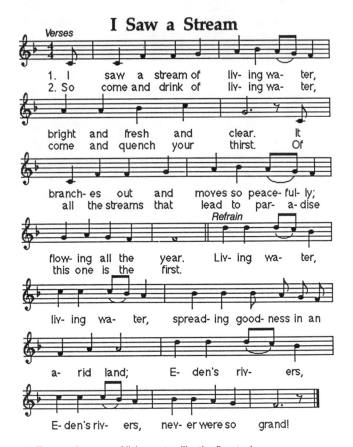

3. The smallest cup of living water, like the finest wine,
   Gives joy and strength and true refreshment; nothing tastes so fine.

4. If you are thirsty for cool water, you must come to him.
   He'll take you to the stream and satisfy all your thirst within.

5. Bend down and taste of living water, you may have your fill.
   You'll go on now for all eternity, longing for it still.

Nablus:
Jacob's Well

Since 636 when the Arabs seized this town due north of Jerusalem, it has been called Nablus. Before that this town was the biblical Shechem. It remains an intensely Islamic city, but with a small colony of Samaritans.

The Samaritan place of sacrifice, Mount Gerizim, is just outside this busy town. On the east slope of the mountain is a walled garden near the highway. Within is an unfinished Greek Orthodox church. Steps lead down to a small chapel which contains the famous well where Jesus sat and talked with the Samaritan woman (John 4: 5-9).

Jacob's well is truly deep — 118 feet. A

Jacob's Well at Nablus

Galilee, Samaria and the Seacoast / 185

monk will pour some water back down and let you wait for the splash. The visitor may also have a drink of the fresh pure water and pause to look at the excellent but expensive icons on sale. Easier on the pocketbook are small pottery jugs filled with — what else? — water from Jacob's well!

Let Us Pray Together

Lord, it was a day of grace for the Samaritan woman from Shechem who met you at this well. She offered you a drink of cool water but you offered her a new life. "If you only knew what God is offering," you said. Would she appreciate this moment? Would she thirst for living water?

Lord, if only we knew what God is offering! If we were only aware of what you offer us when we meet you in our lives, of how you call us to be better, to be challenged and to be changed.

Lord, we thirst for the refreshment that only you can give. Amen.

When the Noonday Sun

1. When the noon-day sun was burn-ing, near a dust-y lit-tle town, Je-sus, wear-y from his jour-ney, by an an-cient well sat down.

2. Came a wo-man to draw wa-ter, a Sa-ma-ri-tan was she; Je-sus thirst-ed for some wa-ter, "Will you give a drink to me?"

3. "How can you, a Jew and stranger, ask a woman such as me
For a drink of cooling water? It's forbidden, don't you see?"

4. "If you knew the gift God's giving, and who asks you for a drink,
You would ask me and I'd give you Living Water here to drink."

5. "Sir, you have no rope or bucket and the well is very deep;
Are you greater than old Jacob when he came here with his sheep?"

6. "Everyone who drinks this water will be thirsty soon again,
But the Water that I'm sharing gives a life that never ends."

Cf. John 4
Folksong from Lothringen
Copyright © 1985 by Willard F. Jabusch

Galilee, Samaria and the Seacoast / 187

Akko
(St. John of Acre)

Acre or Akko is a Mediterranean port which dates back to the Canaanite era. Pilgrims will find that it needs only imagination and money to become a second Jaffa, a place of chic shops, swank galleries, outdoor cafes and restaurants built into the old Crusader warehouses.

In fact, the "gentrification" of old Akko has already begun. There are art exhibits and craft shops there now. Surely, Akko will truly exploit its charm and history someday. But for now this is still a rather seedy but very human town.

Akko has a long history of comings and goings. In 1104, five years after they conquered Jerusalem, the Crusaders took Akko and began a vast building program. They were driven out by the Sultan Saladin in 1187 but King Richard the Lionhearted of England won it back in 1191.

In 1219, a great saint, St. Francis of Assisi, stayed here after he had been given special permission to visit the holy places. St. Francis won the hearts of the Moslems when he tried to bring peace and forgiveness between Islam and Christianity at Damietta in Egypt. Here was a man who came with no sword or armor or greed or pomp. He came barefoot and poor as God's "instrument of peace." After praying at the shrines of Jerusalem and Bethlehem, he stayed with a few of his friars here in Akko.

It was also here that St. Francis heard disturbing news from Italy. Some of the friars were changing his simple rule of life and abandoning "Lady Poverty." It seems likely that Francis wanted to stay in this land where Jesus lived, but

Akko on Mediterranean Sea

it was necessary for him to return to Rome and Assisi to restore to the Friars Minor the ideals of poverty and humility.

Before he boarded the ship, however, Francis dedicated his followers to the care of the holy places. To this day, it is the Franciscans who have the custody of so many churches and shrines associated with the life of Christ. The Franciscans are an international group of volunteers who render a humble and beautiful service to pilgrims of all faiths. Their properties are invariably maintained with dignity and good taste. They themselves are kindly and helpful — worthy followers of the "poor man of Assisi" who came here first in peace and piety.

Let Us Pray Together

Lord Jesus, in the history of Christianity has anyone better understood the meaning of your Gospel than Francis of Assisi? Here at Akko, he longed to stay close to the places where you lived, died and rose. But he was called back to some harsh realities. He had to end his pilgrimage and take up unwelcome responsibilities.

We too will soon be leaving here, O Lord. But may we take with us memories that will nourish us through the years ahead. May our stay here in the Holy Land influence us deeply. Let each of us return home as an instrument of peace, eager to follow the Gospel with courage and gentleness. Amen.

Song of St. Francis

Refrain

Come, my broth-ers, up to now we have done so lit-tle; Come, my sis-ters, now let us be-gin.

Verses

1. Bro-ther Sun with your light and great splen-dor, Sis-ter Moon and stars a-bove, Bro-ther Wind, cloud-y skies and fair weath-er, tell us of our Fa-ther's love.

2. Sis-ter Wa-ter, so pre-cious and hum-ble, Bro-ther Fire, so strong and bright, Mo-ther Earth, who sus-tains us and keeps us, all re-veal God's care and might.

3. Creatures all, give your praise to the Father: Bless my Lord and grateful be;
Give him honor and all benediction; serve him with humility.

4. Francis often reminded the brothers, "Go and preach the gospel word.
Let your life be a sermon of goodness; God in you is seen and heard."

5. "Let the poor see the kindness of Jesus; to the least you have been sent.
May all sinners believe in God's mercy; for the past let all repent."

6. Francis climbed up the hill of La Verna; there the burning seraph came,
Marking him with the wounds of the Savior, sharing Jesus' joy and pain.

7. Francis walked down the road through the valley, through those old and
golden towns;
Meadows bloomed with the flowers of summer; lark and thrush made
joyful sounds.

Mount Carmel: Haifa

At the time of the Crusader kingdom (1099-1187), a certain Brother Brocard and a few others lived near the cave of the Old Testament prophet Elijah on Mount Carmel. Here these contemplatives received a rule of life from Albert, Patriarch of Jerusalem. It marked the "modern" beginning of the Carmelite Order, although Carmelites have always claimed that they were really founded by the Prophet Elijah himself!

Later, a monastery was built on this splendid site. An ornate chapel was built over the famous cave of the Prophet. The monastery enjoys one of the finest views in the Holy Land. The modern port of Haifa is far below and the Mediterranean Sea, always changing in color, stretches out to the west.

Carmelite Monastery, Mount Carmel

Mount Carmel has no New Testament connections, but there are many Old Testament memories. As the cradle of the Carmelite Order, it is quite proper that the great St. Teresa of Avila and St. John of the Cross are honored here. There is also, of course, a statue of Our Lady of Mount Carmel.

In front of the monastery and close to the road is a small memorial. Pilgrims will note that it commemorates the wounded soldiers of Napoleon's army billeted in the monastery during the "Little Corporal's" long and unsuccessful siege of Akko in 1799. When he finally retreated, he left his wounded men behind. They were all slaughtered by the victorious Ahmed Jezzar.

Across the road from the monastery is the famous lighthouse, "Stella Maris" (Star of the Sea). It is named in honor of the Virgin Mary whose statue stands on a tall column. A path leads up the hill to the left of the monastery past some ceramic stations of the cross erected by devout Spaniards. The views are spectacular: the snows of Mt. Hermon to the north, distant Akko, the great bay, and Israel's biggest harbor at your feet. It is a good place to remember all who have died fighting in this beautiful but blood-stained Holy Land. There have been many both before and after the helpless young French soldiers who were massacred here.

Let Us Pray Together

God, Mount Carmel, this fair mountain by the sea has been a place of faith and prayer since the time of Elijah the Prophet. We add our prayers to those who have come here for many centuries. We ask for peace in this land and throughout our world. May cruel wars become only a memory from the past. May all peoples learn to forgive and see each other as brothers and sisters. We ask this in Jesus' name. Amen.

Let Nothing Disturb You

Let noth- ing dis-
turb you Let noth- ing a-
larm you. All pass- es a-
way. God on- ly shall stay, God on- ly shall
stay Pa- tience wins all; for if you have
God, then noth- ing is
want- ing; for if you have
God, then noth- ing is
want- ing, for God is your
all, for God is your all.

Prayer of St. Teresa of Avila
Copyright © 1985 by Willard F. Jabusch

Caesarea Maritima

Caesarea-on-the-sea was named in honor of the emperor Augustus by Herod the Great in 25 B.C. It is now a place of impressive ruins, sunshine and cool winds off the Mediterranean. Summer concerts are given in the ancient Roman theater. And after wandering among the remnants of Greek, Roman and Crusader buildings, there are shops and cafes to visit.

But for Christian pilgrims, Caesarea evokes memories of Pontius Pilate. Pilate resided here and went up to Jerusalem for that fateful Passover. Caesarea was the city where St. Paul was held captive for two years (Acts 23: 25). And it was here that Peter baptized the Roman centurion Cornelius (Acts 10).

But Caesarea continued to be a city of Christian importance. Origen, the famous writer and "Father of the Church" who came from Alexandria, was a teacher here. He founded an important library at Caesarea in the third century. Eusebius, considered the first church historian, was bishop of Caesarea between 313 and 340. Procopius, the great historian at the time of the Emperor Justinian, was also born here about the year 500.

For many centuries, the precious cup which was thought to be the Holy Grail or chalice used by Jesus at the Last Supper was kept here. The Crusader King Baldwin, who considered himself a descendant of Lohengrin, seized it when he occupied the city on May 17, 1101. However, Baldwin was forced to give it to the rulers of

Caesarea's Crusader ruins

Genoa in return for providing ships for the Crusaders' army. The triple apses of the cathedral where the Holy Grail was venerated are still easily seen in Caesarea.

In 1254, King Louis IX of France built the great fortifications and the beautiful Gothic pointed arches in the castle which can still be seen. Marble pillars, broken granite shafts, and fragments of fine carving are in abundant supply. Some of the remains of splendid buildings and monuments can be seen in the waters of the old harbor.

Let Us Pray Together

Lord, on a ship from this harbor of Caesarea, the Apostle Paul set out for Rome and for his trial and execution. He lived and died serving you and the Holy Gospel. Help us to be fearless in defense of what is good and true. Make us aware of what you want us to do with our lives. Make us confident that you live within and give us the strength and hope which we need. "I live now not with my own life but with the life of Christ who lives in me" (Galatians 2: 20). Amen.

Pilgrims visiting the Holy Land

Go Forth To All People

Galilee, Samaria and the Seacoast / 199